PR

"I seriously owe you to the core of me. I just landed a 9.6 million dollar account! I pitched the proposal last week - my phone rings today, it's the business. I wouldn't have had the confidence to pitch that proposal properly if I hadn't been conditioned with your affirmations for the last 20 days" - Becky Alby

"Mantras aren't really my jam but I was very impressed with this book. It exceeded expectations. This was extremely well thought out, the explanations really brought the importance of these statements to life, and it inspired me to make more of a regular habit of this in my life" - Sarah Michelle

"FANTASTIC! It's so much more than an Affirmation book. The very wise and profound comments about each one are very valuable and bring the Affirmations to life in a significant way. I felt a lovely shift in my Money Mindset" - Minda Burr

"I absolutely loved it. I was able to shed so much negative baggage such as shame for the financial decisions I've made. I feel empowered, inspired and not alone. I would recommend it to everyone" - Yvonne Heath

31 BAD A$$

MONEY MINDSET AFFIRMATIONS

A month to train your subconscious into easily building wealth and abundance

WITH

JOYCE ROJAS

www.joycerojas.com

First Edition

ISBN: 978-1-7367353-1-2

This book is written from my perspective based on my experience and knowledge. It is not meant to give personalized financial or investment advice and is not endorsed by my past or present employers. Names and stories have been modified to protect privacy.

Cover and Interior Design: Margaret Cogswell
Cover Photo: Cristal Rojas
Editor: Rusti Lehay

To my son
who has given my life meaning and whom
I love more than anything in this world,
my mom
whose love is inexhaustible,
my dad
who is still my superhero,
my siblings
who fill my life with laughter,
God
for the never-ending
help & guidance,
and to
YOU the reader –
I see you, I feel you, I'm with you.

31 BADASS MONEY MINDSET AFFIRMATIONS

"I'm going to do a terrific show today...because I'm good enough, I'm smart enough, and doggonit, people like me!"

If you know where the above quote is from, then your first impression of affirmations is similar to mine. In his chunky pastel blue grandpa sweater, perfectly combed hair parted to one side and a comical lispy voice, Stuart Smalley from Saturday Night Live would repeat this affirmation in the mirror before starting a show. What made it hilarious was how dorky he looked and sounded reciting his affirmations. That was my first impression of affirmations; I thought they were lame, and something used by people with low self-esteem. It was not my kinda thing, you know? I was cooler than that. Little did I know that decades later, I'd be using affirmations to help me during one of the lowest points of my life.

My life drastically changed by using the power of affirmations, but my affirmations weren't Stuart Smalley style. I didn't say them in the mirror or block out a particular time of the day to do them. They were simply the thoughts I would assert in my mind over and over again. Affirmations are essentially the self-talk we choose to give ourselves. We all have self-talk but it's typically the crappy kind – we say things like, "this kinda sh*t always happens to me... if I have any luck, it's bad luck... I'm not good with numbers... I'm fat... I can't do this... I'm old... I'm broke... same shit different day." All of these thoughts and sayings are essentially 'affirmations' except they're affirming the negative things we see in ourselves and our lives rather than the positive! We want to program our minds with positive affirmations like, "the world works in my favor... I am so blessed.... I am financially free... I am beautiful... I can do anything I set my mind to... I am young and vibrant... I am abundant... I am f*cking amazing!" Not only does this type of programming inspire and empower us, it also changes our biology.

Imagine your brain as a forest and every thought you have creates its own little pathway in the forest of your brain. The more you think that thought, the more that pathway expands, and soon it becomes a clear and familiar path you take often. Most of us continue taking the same path day in and day out - or in other words, most of us think the same damn thoughts every day and end up getting the same results. We then wonder, "Why do I feel stagnant in life? Why am I not growing wealth? Why is my business/career not growing?" I have an answer for you: because you keep taking the *same pathway*, having the *same* thoughts, which then yield the same results! You're also very likely thinking the wrong kind of thoughts and the pathway you're expanding in your mind is working against you rather than for you.

The affirmations and exercises in this book will challenge you to change your old ordinary thoughts to new powerful thoughts. This shift in thoughts will then change your actions thereby changing your results and inevitably leading you to success. This is a profound mindset shift... BUT buyer beware, it *will* feel uncomfortable because, after all, you are changing your biology! Your new thoughts are rewiring your brain – you are making new pathways in the forest of your brain and it's uncomfortable to cut through untrodden territory.

Science has proven that there is an undeniable, powerful connection between our thoughts and our physical bodies. For example, the placebo effect demonstrates how thoughts can directly impact health. A person is told they've been given a medication that will alleviate or cure their illness and the person then feels better, yet in reality they were only given a sugar pill. Similarly, doctors have run experiments where patients are made to believe they've had a surgery (which they did not actually have), yet somehow the patients feel better and move better. How is this possible if it was a fake surgery? This is the power of thought at work.

Every thought you have causes temporary or lasting neurochemical changes in your brain as connections between neurons are being forged. Most people don't challenge their daily thought patterns, habits and behaviors and, as a result, the same pathways are consistently being used. However, if we shift our thoughts, new pathways are created, and the brain is changed. You are changing your neurochemistry when you change your thoughts. You are actively choosing to change your biology! This is called self-directed neuroplasticity – it's your ability to change your mind any way you'd like! *You are re-creating yourself, and if you're powerful enough to change your biology, you're powerful enough to change your life.*

How your thoughts dictate your wealth

In almost 20 years of working with people in the banking and investment industry as a financial advisor and a leader, I've learned there was much more to wealth than just financial knowledge. Many financial gurus, advisors and literacy programs give knowledge but fail to teach you the mindset needed to become wealthy. Let's face it, if you really wanted to learn how to be rich you can google that sh*t and make it happen but judging from the fact that over 50% of people live paycheck to paycheck, I'm going to go out on a limb and conclude that financial knowledge does not equal wealth. This is especially true if you grew up in a low to moderate income family or a family with fear-based or limiting beliefs around money, like I did. Don't believe me? Check out studies showing that lottery winners are more likely than the average American to declare bankruptcy within 3 to 5 years. Wait...what?! But they just won the lottery, how'd they go bankrupt so quickly??! They are reacting to the financial thermostat in their subconscious mind.

We all have a financial thermostat in our subconscious minds programmed at a certain level of wealth and success. We feel comfortable at this 'temperature' and will stay there unless we actively choose to change it. So, if you're wondering why you can't break through a certain salary level or can't seem to grow your savings, don't blame your kids or job – it's time to check within yourself.

I was forced to check within myself when I ended up a broke single mom losing my house in the midst of a recession and a heartbreaking divorce. I remember selling all of my belongings for pennies on the dollar in a garage sale: the race-car-shaped bed I had tucked my son into for years, the patio bistro set I loved to sit on while drinking my morning coffee, the rubber ducky bathroom décor that my son loved... I sold it all and with every piece sold, I felt like a failure. I had failed my marriage, my son, my parents, my religious beliefs, but mostly I had failed myself. I had expected more from myself and from life. I felt I was capable of more. Somewhere deep inside I knew this, but I just couldn't see it and I definitely wasn't living it. I wanted to cry inconsolably. I wanted to scream out loud. Loud enough for God to hear me screaming that this wasn't f*cking fair, that this wasn't the way things were supposed to go...but I couldn't because there was a beautiful boy looking to me for hope and direction. I remember struggling to hold the tears back as my son and I left our home and packed the car. I looked at my son's beautiful big brown eyes, I could see he was scared but suddenly a smile came over his face as he asked "We're going on an adventure, right mom?"

"Yes, honey!" I replied with a nervous smile, "a BIG adventure!"

Truth is, I had no idea what I was doing, how I was going to get through this or what the future held for us. Awful thoughts of everything that could go wrong filled my head every day. It was during this time that I began using affirmations without even knowing I was using them. I wouldn't say them in the mirror, aloud, or have a script. I would simply catch myself thinking negative thoughts and I'd reverse them into hopeful thoughts. I would repeat these faith-filled thoughts in my head over and over again, especially during times where I doubted myself or felt fear over what could go wrong. It was a way to coach myself into believing that I was powerful, smart and strong enough to get through anything. They worked! Less than 5 years later, I quadrupled my income & assets, I got my Masters in Business Administration, spent more time with my son, aligned myself with my purpose, and was happier, more alive than I had ever been. What caused this drastic change? ***The moment I began to change my thoughts, I changed my reality.***

Your belief system plays a huge part in how you handle money. Studies show that 95% of what we do every day is based on our subconscious and only 5% is conscious. That means that your subconscious is what's truly calling the shots in your decision making and creating what you see in your life today. *Subconscious beliefs programmed in your mind when you were a child are making financial decisions for you now, in your adult life.* Isn't that crazy? Would you have a 7-year-old child run your business? Would you hire a 7-year-old as a financial advisor to plan your retirement? I don't think so, yet the 7-year-old you is actively making decisions in your financial life today based on your childhood fears and insecurities. It's what I call your money story.

What's Your Money Story?

Your money story consists of various experiences in your past that have programmed certain beliefs into your mind. These beliefs can be around money, yourself, or the world and they continue to play out into your adult life. Your money story seeps into different areas of your life – relationships, career, and health – because at the end of the day, money is involved in just about everything. Your money story is at play in your subconscious whenever you make decisions both big and small: which college to choose, what to study, what job to take, what to do with your money, who to marry, where to live, and the list goes on.

When I delved into my personal money story, I realized all my money challenges had been inevitable. I grew up in a low-income household, daughter of immigrant parents, my mom didn't have a voice in financial decisions, I never learned about investing because my dad was too scared to lose the little he had, and I saw my dad work so hard to make money so I believed working hard was the only way to build wealth. This money story was the perfect recipe for a disastrous money mindset. It was only a matter of time before my subconscious belief system caught up with me. It's no surprise that I went from being a poor Latina Jersey girl to a broke single mom. Given my subconscious belief systems, it was inevitable that I'd make bad financial decisions like buying a home at the peak of the market, choosing a partner that was financially unstable, and staying stuck within an income ceiling. Every step of the way was designed and created by my subconscious belief system because being broke was familiar to me. My mind was creating everything I subconsciously expected from myself, money and the world; the same way your mind is creating everything you subconsciously expect.

In this book, I'll share affirmations that will reprogram your subconscious. I will instill positive money beliefs designed to inform, awaken, and empower you so that you can take control of your finances and live in abundance. I will also take you through exercises designed to develop your awareness of belief systems that may be holding you back, recognize important parts of your financial picture, and take actionable steps to help you thrive financially without working so damn hard for it. Let's get the party started!

How to successfully use this book

There are 31 affirmations in this book, 1 for each day of the month, to start your day with a positive outlook on yourself, the world, and your finances. It takes at least between 22 and 66 days to reprogram your subconscious, so make an effort to commit for a consecutive 31 days. Ready to create some magic in your money life? Here's the magical formula to make it happen:

1. Read 1 affirmation per day and the explanation behind it for 31 consecutive days.

If you miss a day, it's okay, just pick up where you left off. However, challenge yourself to do 31 consecutive days because that's how you rewire your brain.

There is a 'Comfort Rating' area at the end of each affirmation. Jot down how comfortable this affirmation was to you on a scale from 1 to 10.

1 being very uncomfortable where you may be thinking, "I feel like this is complete bullsh*t."

10 being "Yes! I love this! I'm vibing with this baby."

2. Say the affirmation aloud.

Say it aloud at least 20 times with feeling. Feel it and visualize it. An easy way to do this is to fantasize about this affirmation being true in your life today. How would it feel to be living that right now? Feel that feeling now. Allow yourself to daydream and feel as if you were a kid again. If you want it to go even deeper, continue to repeat it in your head during the day, while you drive, walk, commute, or frolic around the house.

3. Do the exercise.

(Seriously, do the damn exercise!) The exercises are designed to tap into your subconscious beliefs, bring some money blocks to light, brainstorm ideas for your future, and connect you to your finances in a non-threatening way.

Enjoy as your financial life begins to positively change!

Extra Magic

For some extra magic, record the affirmations on a voice memo in your phone. In Dr. Bruce Lipton's book *Biology of Belief*[1], he says the subconscious learns through hypnosis and repetition. You can do both of those with this book and a voice memo on your phone! If you record the affirmations on a voice memo, you can play them during the day and repeat along so that your subconscious will begin to accept it and your conscious creative mind will begin to figure out a way to make it happen. Another idea is to use that recording as a wake-up alarm so that it's the first thing you hear in the morning. At night, you can auto hypnotize yourself by listening to these affirmations as you go to sleep because that's when your brain is in theta and open to hypnosis. You can also purchase the audio version of this book and listen to it as you go about your day – even having it play in the background will help your subconscious with some healthy thoughts. These tips help the affirmations permeate your subconscious and begin replacing old belief systems faster.

[1] Lipton, B.(2005.) *The Biology of Belief: Unleashing the Power of Consciousness, Matter and Miracles* (1st ed.). Mountain of Love

Challenges You May Come Across

"This affirmation is just not resonating with me."

Not every affirmation will resonate or feel 'right'. One reason may be because it might not be a challenge you're currently facing. However, don't be fooled. What I found in my focus group was that the people who claimed the affirmation 'didn't resonate' with them were the ones that direly needed that affirmation. For example, there were a handful of people that claimed certain affirmations didn't sit well with them and when I dug deeper, I found that the type of affirmations they were having trouble with, were for self-love. These same people had admitted to struggling with self-esteem and confidence; therefore, their minds were resisting the self-love affirmations and that's why it 'wasn't resonating'.

The subconscious mind resists change, so to change it, you'll need to introduce new thoughts and take new actions habitually. You are accomplishing both these requirements by being consistent with these daily affirmations. Additionally, the exercises guide your conscious mind to come up with action steps that will create this new 'reality' that the subconscious is now being introduced to via the affirmations.

"I feel like I'm lying to myself."

When you affirm something that you don't see proof of in your current reality, you're going to feel like you're lying to yourself. Remember, the purpose of affirmations is to give your brain a directive of where you want to go, so naturally these affirmations will challenge your current reality – they're supposed to! However, if it feels too 'untrue' or you find yourself not even being able to imagine the state that the affirmation asserts, you can tweak it by using words such as: I am open to, I am capable of, I can, I choose.

Handy Dandy Examples:

ORIGINAL AFFIRMATION: "Every financial decision I make multiplies my income."

YOU: "No, it doesn't! My decisions are awful! I'm trying to say this, but I feel like I'm lying."

THE TWEAK: Every financial decision I make *can* multiply my income.

ORIGINAL AFFIRMATION: I am a sexy, smart money-making machine.

YOU: "I don't feel comfortable saying that. I don't feel sexy, I've never been sexy, I just don't like this affirmation - it sucks."

THE TWEAK: I am capable of being a sexy, smart money-making machine.

I am open to being a sexy, smart money-making machine.

You can tweak it FOR NOW, but at some point, you're going to have to buckle down and practice the original affirmation in order to challenge your mindset. Otherwise, what's the point of this book? It's definitely not to leave you with the same thinking you had before reading it, so challenge your mind and subconscious to see yourself in a different light. As you repeat these affirmations, they begin to create a footprint in your subconscious so that as time goes on, it becomes easier for you to accept what you're affirming. Your inner reality is changing and soon, your outer reality will match.

"I don't have the time" or "I forget!"

Seriously? Do you seriously want to use this lame excuse to procrastinate your success? Is this the excuse you'll use to shove away your greatness? As a single mom with side hustles and a full-time job, I'll keep it real with you and say "If I could find time to say these affirmations, so can you." It only takes 10 minutes (if that). Decide NOW: At what time of your day will you accomplish these affirmations? As soon as you wake up? Before going to sleep? While you drive? On your lunch break? Before touching social media every day? While you shower? **What 10 minutes do you want to dedicate towards your mental and financial wealth?**

If you 'don't have time' to create financial freedom for yourself and your family, create a life you truly want, and give yourself mental peace around your money life, then you just don't want it badly enough. Gift this book to someone who's ready for it. I know, it sounds harsh but I refuse to baby you or give into excuses, and you shouldn't either. Excuses are RESISTANCE creeping in. It's your brain not wanting change because it likes familiarity and it knows how to handle what it's already seen, heard, and experienced. The moment you give it something new to do, your brain resists because it doesn't know whether it's a good change or a bad one. Fight through this and say your damn affirmations!

YOUR TURN:

I commit to accomplish my affirmations during this part of my day:

____

____

____

I want to practice these affirmations because I want them to help me...(What change is it that you want to see in your life?)

____

____

____

____

____

____

IT'S AFFIRMATION TIME!

1

DATE ____________________

I AM A *Creator* AND *Everything* I TOUCH PROSPERS

If you think that your life is created by the people and circumstances around you – your boss, parents, partners, government, society, race, income level etc. – you are in denial of your own power. It is time to recognize and embrace that YOU are a magical being. You are one with God and the Universe. You are a creator. Understand and accept that. It is YOU creating your life. It is you who makes choices, takes action and chooses your reactions. You can create prosperity, happiness and abundance in your life *if* and *when* you choose to. There will be times in life when you feel you're not prospering but remember that seeds take time to grow. No sturdy tree grows overnight. Keep taking action, believe, and be ready to receive because what you choose to create *will* prosper.

I am a Creator and everything I touch prospers
I am a Creator and everything I touch prospers
I am a Creator and everything I touch prospers
...Repeat 20 times

COMFORT RATING		**1=** This is complete bullsh*t **10=** I love this! I'm vibing with this, baby!

YOUR TURN:

You are a creator so think about what you'd like to create in these 8 areas of life and write it down. It doesn't matter if it doesn't seem 'realistic' or you're not living it right now – just write down what you *want* to create.

FINANCES ______________________________

____

____

____

____

____

____

____

RELATIONSHIPS __________________________

____

____

____

____

____

____

____

SPIRITUAL/PERSONAL GROWTH_______________

____

____

____

____

CAREER

FUN

HEALTH

LEGACY

ENVIRONMENT

NOTES

I Know WHAT I WANT AND I Confidently TAKE INSPIRED ACTION

When you get into your car, you've already decided where you're going right? Do this with life – decide what you want. If you're unclear or indecisive, you are living life by default because others end up making decisions for you. To create the life you want, be clear and decisive on *what* you want.

So, imagine being in your car and knowing where you want to go, what's the next step? Turn the car on. That is 1 little action step but a very important one. It's the same with life, just take 1 step towards what you want and trust that the next step will become clearer as you move forward.

Now your car is running and instead of wasting time wondering 'how do I get there?', you turn on your navigation system. It's the same with life – you have internal and external navigation systems at your disposal. Your internal navigation systems are logic and intuition.

COMFORT RATING

1= This is complete bullsh*t
10= I love this! I'm vibing with this, baby!

Your external navigation systems are mentors, coaches, teachers and people that have already accomplished what you want to do. The key to driving life is to decide, act, and keep moving.

I know what I want, and I confidently take inspired action
I know what I want, and I confidently take inspired action
I know what I want, and I confidently take inspired action
...Repeat 20 times

YOUR TURN:

Create a clear picture of what you want your financial life to look like.

How much do I want to make?

____

____

Why?____________________________________

____

____

____

____

____

____

____

____

____

____

How much do I want to have in savings, investments, real estate?

What for?

What coaches, professionals, or partners do I want involved in my finances?

NOTES

DATE ____________________

MONEY COMES TO ME *Easily* AND *Frequently*

Think back to your childhood – what were some of the things you learned about money? Many of us saw, heard or experienced our parents have money problems. We may have heard false statements like:

"We can't afford it."
"You need to work hard for your money."
"Money doesn't grow on trees."
"Money is the root of all evil."
"Money is for necessities only."
"Money doesn't come easy."

All of these statements are limiting beliefs passed on from generation to generation. They sow the seed of limitation in your mind, creating a negative reality about money without you even noticing. It's time to sow seeds of abundance into your subconscious and therefore into your life. With this book, you will begin to embrace the reality that money is easy to create and manifest. You will begin to see changes in your financial

COMFORT RATING		**1=** This is complete bullsh*t **10=** I love this! I'm vibing with this, baby!

life because your mindset has shifted into attracting and manifesting abundance. You can take this mindset and pass it on to your children too so that generational financial abundance is carried on.

Money comes to me easily and frequently
Money comes to me easily and frequently
Money comes to me easily and frequently
...Repeat 20 times

YOUR TURN:

What did you see, hear, and experience with money as a child?

What are your current stressors around money?

What possible links or patterns do you see between your past experiences and your present?

NOTES

DATE ____________________

4
I AM Designed FOR ABUNDANCE AND Prosperity

It's time to recognize that you live in an abundant universe. Check out my girl, Mother Nature – you give her 1 seed and she begins to create and prosper. Trees grow as tall as they can, fruit is produced in multitudes, blades of grass grow anywhere they can survive even in between the cracks of concrete. Why? Because Mother Nature is naturally abundant and prosperous. YOU, my friend, are part of nature! It is in your core to be abundant and prosperous. Your body is designed to be at peak performance as long as you treat it well. Your mind wants to learn more, your soul craves to expand in consciousness.

You are designed for abundance, growth, and prosperity and your finances are part of that. Don't feel guilty for wanting abundance, it's natural. Accept that you were made to be abundant and that you desire to be in your natural state. Don't trick yourself into thinking you lack

COMFORT RATING		**1=** This is complete bullsh*t **10=** I love this! I'm vibing with this, baby!

W

the skills, knowledge, or ability to prosper. Accept that there are seeds of greatness in you *right now* – you are already prospering. The power to create abundance and prosperity in your world is *already in you* and it is time to tap into it.

I am designed for abundance and prosperity
I am designed for abundance and prosperity
I am designed for abundance and prosperity
...Repeat 20 times

YOUR TURN:

List 10 experiences, visions, or goals in the past that you set out to achieve and successfully accomplished.

1.____

2.____

3.____

4.

5.

6.

7.

8.

9.

10.

These are all proof of your ability to create abundance and prosperity!

NOTES

DATE ____________________

I Trust THAT Everything WORKS IN MY FAVOR

I remember leaving California in the midst of a recession with only my kid, my car and a cooler in the backseat. I had lost my house, my marriage, my confidence and myself. I was heartbroken and as I drove, I'd let the tears run down my face only when my son was sleeping so that he wouldn't see my pain. I had no idea what I was doing – all I knew was that I had to do this and would fill in the blanks as I went along. The one thing I'd repeat to myself over and over again is "everything works in my favor, everything works in my favor, everything works in my favor." This affirmation changed my fear into strength and my tears into hope. A few years later, I succeeded in quadrupling my income and assets, got my master's in business administration, and was spending more time with my son than ever before. I don't know if I would've been able to make it through this time in my life without this affirmation.

The Universe works *with you* to create what you want. It works with you, even if at times it feels like it's working

COMFORT RATING

1= This is complete bullsh*t
10= I love this! I'm vibing with this, baby!

against you. When you are in motion, the universe begins to move with you – it picks up your thoughts, feelings, and energy which is why it's important to guard your thoughts and to focus on what you want in life, not what you fear. Trust that everything is working for you, not against you. If you trust in this, you will begin to realize how experiences that had seemed bad in the past were actually part of the design to promote and grow you because everything works in your favor.

I trust that everything works in my favor
I trust that everything works in my favor
I trust that everything works in my favor
...Repeat 20 times

YOUR TURN:

Write about a past experience that felt bad at the moment but ended up somehow working in your favor.

____

____

____

____

____

____

____

____

____

____

NOTES

DATE ____________________

I AM FULLY *Open* TO RECEIVING *Wealth* AND *Abundance*

You may logically say that you want wealth but subconsciously you may be blocking it. There are 3 mindset factors that can affect your abundance:

1. The way you feel about yourself
2. The way you feel about the world
3. The way you feel about money

The way you see these 3 things can determine your level of abundance. Let's break it down: If you don't truly love yourself, you won't truly accept abundance because something inside of you feels that you don't deserve it. If you don't trust the world, you'll be suspicious of anything good that shows up because who accepts gifts from an entity they don't trust? If you don't believe others are here to help you, you won't notice the opportunities people bring you. If you have something against money, you're not going to want much of it.

COMFORT RATING		**1=** This is complete bullsh*t **10=** I love this! I'm vibing with this, baby!

If you shift your mindset around these 3 things, abundance will be easier. Wealth and abundance are all around you if you open yourself up to receiving it in the various forms it shows up. Begin to see the little ways that abundance is offering itself up to you – the people that offer you help, the coincidences in life, the coins you find on the floor, the affection you receive – are all abundance speaking to you in different languages. Be open, believe, and receive.

I am fully open to receiving wealth and abundance
I am fully open to receiving wealth and abundance
I am fully open to receiving wealth and abundance
...Repeat 20 times

YOUR TURN:

How has abundance showed up for you this past week? List at least 5 ways. If you can't come up with anything, think harder!

1.______________________________

____

____

____

____

____

2.______________________________

____

3.

4.

5.

NOTES

7

DATE ____________________

I AM IN *Complete* POWER. MONEY NEEDS *Me.* MONEY WANTS *Me.*

We've been taught to chase money and this idea is wrong. When we chase money, we place the power in *money*, when in reality, we are the ones in power. Money doesn't have any meaning without us in the picture. We are the creators of products and services, money is just what's being exchanged for what we have to offer. Let's break this concept down even further...the average hours a human has per lifetime, if they live until 80 years old, is 700,800 hours (365 days x 24 hours x 80 years). BUT, if you like to eat, sleep, and poop, then that leaves you with only about 408,800 hours, or 14 hours per day. You may be thinking "that's still a lot of hours!" But wait, let's deduct time for the average American's activities:

14 hours – 8 hours for work – 1 hour commute – 4 hours TV time – 2 hours social media = **–1 hour**

We're actually negative 1 hour! We typically deduct this from sleep, time with our family, or self care. If this were a bank account, we would have overdrawn our account, but because it's 'just our time,' we don't notice it. We fail to realize that we've been allotted a limited number of

COMFORT RATING		**1=** This is complete bullsh*t **10=** I love this! I'm vibing with this, baby!

hours on this earth, so every activity in our day is being exchanged for life energy in our life bank account. When we go to work, a company pays us *in exchange for* our life energy. When we spend time with a client, they are paying for our life energy. When we watch TV, we use our life energy. So what is the real asset here? Is it money or is it YOU? It's YOU. *Time is the 1 thing we cannot buy and every day that passes, we must wisely choose what to trade our precious hours for.*

After speaking at a women's conference, I received so many messages on how this mindset shift had changed their lives. One entrepreneur shared, "My income increased and business expanded because of your talk. I was undercharging for my services and you helped me realize that." Another expressed, "Every time I spend money now, I realize that it's costing me the energetic exchange of my life hours. The less I spend, the less I have to work, thus the more time I can spend with my kids."

Life's short. We think we're here for a long time, think we'll have tomorrow to do that 'thing' we've been putting off, think we'll have that person in our life tomorrow to tell them what we didn't tell them today... but *nothing* is promised. Everything and everyone in your life right now is only lent to you, so make sure you are using your time and money for what you value the most. This is true financial freedom.

I am in complete power. Money needs me, money wants me.
I am in complete power. Money needs me, money wants me.
I am in complete power. Money needs me, money wants me.
...Repeat 20 times

YOUR TURN:

Take inventory of your time. Below you'll find a chart. Plot what you do with your time in this schedule. Try to account for as much of your time as you can. List the time you typically take, what you're doing, how it makes you feel, and whether that feeling is positive, negative or neutral.

ACTIVITY	LENGTH OF TIME	😃 😐 ☹️

NOTES

DATE ___________________

I AM A *Sexy,* SMART *Money-Making* MACHINE

Yes, it's possible to be sexy, successful, and intelligent all in ONE package! And guess where that package is? That's right! It's YOU! YOU are intelligent and successful enough to make your visions come true...and you know what? That's pretty damn sexy! Allow yourself to be the best version of You. Give yourself permission to shine brightly, to push the barriers holding you back, to be that image of yourself you see in your mind but are afraid to tap into. Do not dim your power by depending on someone else for money, attention, or love because everything you need is already within YOU. It is time to be the game changer you were meant to be. You are smart, powerful and sexy enough to create the life you want, and the time is NOW.

P.S. If this affirmation made you feel a little uncomfortable, ask yourself, "Why?" Some of us have challenges seeing ourselves as sexy or successful because we base our definitions on society's standards, not our own. YOU

COMFORT RATING

1= This is complete bullsh*t
10= I love this! I'm vibing with this, baby!

define what 'sexy' is. YOU define what being 'successful' means to you. Do not hold yourself to standards created by others. Create your own.

I am a sexy, smart money-making machine
I am a sexy, smart money-making machine
I am a sexy, smart money-making machine
...Repeat 20 times

YOUR TURN:

What does "success" mean to you?

____
____
____
____
____
____

What does being 'sexy' mean to you?

____
____
____
____
____
____
____

When do you feel the sexiest and the most powerful around money?

____

____

____

____

____

____

____

____

What three steps can you take to cultivate more of that feeling and way of 'being'?

1.______________________________________

____

____

____

____

2. ______________________________________

____

____

____

____

3.______________________________________

____

____

____

NOTES

9

DATE ____________________

I AM A *Master* OF *Wealth* AND SUCCESS

My parents emigrated from Ecuador, so I was the first generation to be born in the USA. My dad worked really hard to provide for 4 of us little leeches and it still felt like there wasn't enough. We got 1 pair of shoes and jeans per year, weren't allowed to go to birthday parties or participate in secret santas because we couldn't afford a gift, and no class field trips for me. "We can't afford it!" was engraved into my brain so much that somewhere along the way, my child subconscious decided that this was where I belonged. I was a poor girl from immigrant parents and always would be. It took me over a decade to break this limiting subconscious belief system and adopt new ones to help me succeed.

Your mind can sentence you to settling for less in life or can inspire you to expect more. Our subconscious belief system, which was mostly created in our childhood, plays a big role in the decisions we make today. The sneaky thing is that we don't even notice it because we catch our conscious thoughts, but not the subconscious. You may think "I don't have any limiting beliefs" but

COMFORT RATING		**1=** This is complete bullsh*t **10=** I love this! I'm vibing with this, baby!

that's your conscious mind speaking. The work of your subconscious mind can be seen in what you've created thus far in your life. If you're not financially where you want to be, something is holding you back and it is very likely lurking in a dark corner of your subconscious mind. But the good news is that you could find them and change them. Awareness of negative subconscious beliefs is the first step to releasing them. The next step is to switch the script and that's what you're doing with these affirmations, fam!

I am a master of wealth and success
I am a master of wealth and success
I am a master of wealth and success
...Repeat 20 times

YOUR TURN:

Let's go subconscious belief hunting...
Set a one minute timer to finish each of these sentences. Do not stop writing/typing for the entire minute. Use one minute for each sentence.

Money is.... ______________________________________

____

____

____

____

____

____

In my life, money.... ______________________________

People with money.... ______________________________

More money means....

NOTES

10

DATE ______________________

EVERY *Financial* DECISION I MAKE *Multiplies* MY INCOME

If you're scared or uncomfortable making financial decisions, it's probably because you're lying to yourself in some way, shape or form. Maybe you tell yourself you're not good with money, don't have enough experience, or keep thinking about past financial mistakes you've made. These thoughts begin to haunt you and become limiting beliefs that lurk in the dark corners of your brain. Do not let them take root! Change those thoughts now because the longer you stay in this cycle of self-doubt and fear, the longer it will take you to build wealth. Begin to confidently control your finances by repeating this affirmation and by taking steps to understand your numbers, finding mentorship, and taking small, calculated risks. You are savvy and intuitive enough to make prosperous decisions. If you need assistance, the universe is filled with mentors and advisors ready to guide you.

I remember when Karen came to me, she said "My father left me a lot of money. He was great at finances

COMFORT RATING		**1=** This is complete bullsh*t **10=** I love this! I'm vibing with this, baby!

but never taught me anything about it. I don't know what I'm doing and I need your help." I noticed her lack of confidence in money decisions; any time she needed to make a decision about her finances, she would get nervous and frustrated. One day, with tears in her eyes, she exasperatingly said, "I feel so stupid!" I lovingly reminded her of all the decisions she had made with her money up until now. "Actually, you've done a great job," I said, "it's *you* who chose to come and make sure your finances are on track. *You* decided how much risk to take on your investments. *You* helped me come up with a monthly budget for you. *You* chose to work with me. These are all your decisions that have led you to financial security. It's not me, it's *you*. I'm only here as a guide". "I guess you're right," she said with a smile. After that day she didn't get as nervous around money as she had in the past and began to gain confidence in her ability to make sound financial decisions.

Every financial decision I make multiplies my income
Every financial decision I make multiplies my income
Every financial decision I make multiplies my income
...Repeat 20 times

YOUR TURN:

Not all financial decisions you've made have been a sh*t show – there must have been great financial decisions you've made in the past. Find at least 5 of those moments and write them down.

1.____

____

2.

3.

4.

5.

NOTES

11

DATE ____________________

I Love MONEY AND Money LOVES ME

When was the last time you said, "Damn, I looooovee Money!"? If you have, you've probably gotten some ugly stares or people telling you that, "Money isn't everything," "we shouldn't love money because it makes us greedy," blah, blah, blah. All false. Many of us have been led to believe that loving money is a bad thing. Meanwhile, for some reason, it's okay to say, "I love happy hour!" without being seen as a drunk, "I love pizza" without being labeled a glutton, "I love this dress" without being accused of being a materialistic brat. But if you say, "I love money" you're labeled as greedy? Give me a break!

You can love money, the same way you love your dog, fresh baked chocolate chip cookies, or cuddling up to a Netflix movie on a lazy Sunday. Release the negative connotation placed around money by understanding that it is a wonderful tool to help you create the experiences you desire in life. All those experiences I just mentioned - the dog, netflix and cookies - they all cost money, no? If you have a negative viewpoint of money,

COMFORT RATING		**1=** This is complete bullsh*t **10=** I love this! I'm vibing with this, baby!

then subconsciously you won't want it and energetically you won't attract it. You gotta love money so that money can love you back. This puts a positive energetic frequency around money rather than making it taboo. I'm not asking you to make love to hundred-dollar bills (unless you want to), but I need you to see the silliness around the idea that you shouldn't love money.

I love money and money loves me
I love money and money loves me
I love money and money loves me
...Repeat 20 times

YOUR TURN:

Use the table to write down 5 experiences on your bucket list. Calculate how much each of these experiences will cost. (If you don't know, find out!) By when would you like to make each of those happen?

EXPERIENCE	COST	BY WHEN?

NOTES

DATE ____________________

I AM RESPONSIBLE AND *Purposeful* WITH MY *Money*

I know, I know...this affirmation sounds a bit boring - like, "Seriously? Now I need to find a purpose for my money??" But here's the deal, spending money frivolously does not lead to wealth, instead it leads to the creation of a pattern that becomes a bad habit. Spending is typically emotionally charged - it is used to create or get rid of an emotion. Have you ever snacked on food just because you're bored, anxious, or stressed? I'm sure you have, and your spending patterns are similar. Many people use spending for feelings of comfort, achievement, validation, or instant gratification. If you begin noticing what you feel when you spend, you'll find your emotional spending pattern. Do you spend when you're bored, upset, sad, excited, or need change in your life? Do you like the feeling of getting several little amazon packages at your doorstep because it excites you? Dig deeper into the emotion of your purchases because that could help you break a pattern that's holding you back.

COMFORT RATING		**1=** This is complete bullsh*t **10=** I love this! I'm vibing with this, baby!

Terrence's dream was to buy a house, but he was in a lot of debt so that dream seemed far away. I asked him to bring me 3 months of his credit card statements, and as I poured through them, I found a pattern. He spent money taking family and friends out. "What feeling does this give you?" I asked him. "I love spending time with my friends and family. I feel closeness and love," he responded. "How can you do this without going out as much?" I asked. He began inviting them over to his apartment instead. Only 1 year later, Terrence had saved enough to buy a new house.

Give your money purpose based on what you want to create in your life. For example, a portion of your money can be used for monthly responsibilities like mortgage, rent, food and utilities. A separate portion can be for a future investment property or start-up business. Another portion can be a 'fun fund' for vacation, shopping, etc. This aims your money based on the direction you want your life to take rather than letting your emotional patterns take charge.

I am responsible and purposeful with my money
I am responsible and purposeful with my money
I am responsible and purposeful with my money
...Repeat 20 times

YOUR TURN:

Let's put your money into Purpose Buckets. On the next page you'll find 4 fund buckets:

1. CUSHION FUND = what you have in cash, checking & savings accounts. It's used for emergency purposes and for monthly bills.

2. SHORT TERM = money set aside for a goal taking place between 2 and 4 years like buying a house, paying for a kid's over-exaggerated tuition, or buying a business

3. LONG TERM = holds money you'll use 5 years or later like retirement funds or college planning.

4. FUN FUND = money you have set aside for vacations, weekends out with friends, taking the kids to an amusement park, etc.

Fill in how much you currently have in your buckets. If your money isn't structured this way, it's okay, you're not alone. Just fill in how much you intend to have in each bucket now that you will be purposeful with your money.

FUND BUCKETS

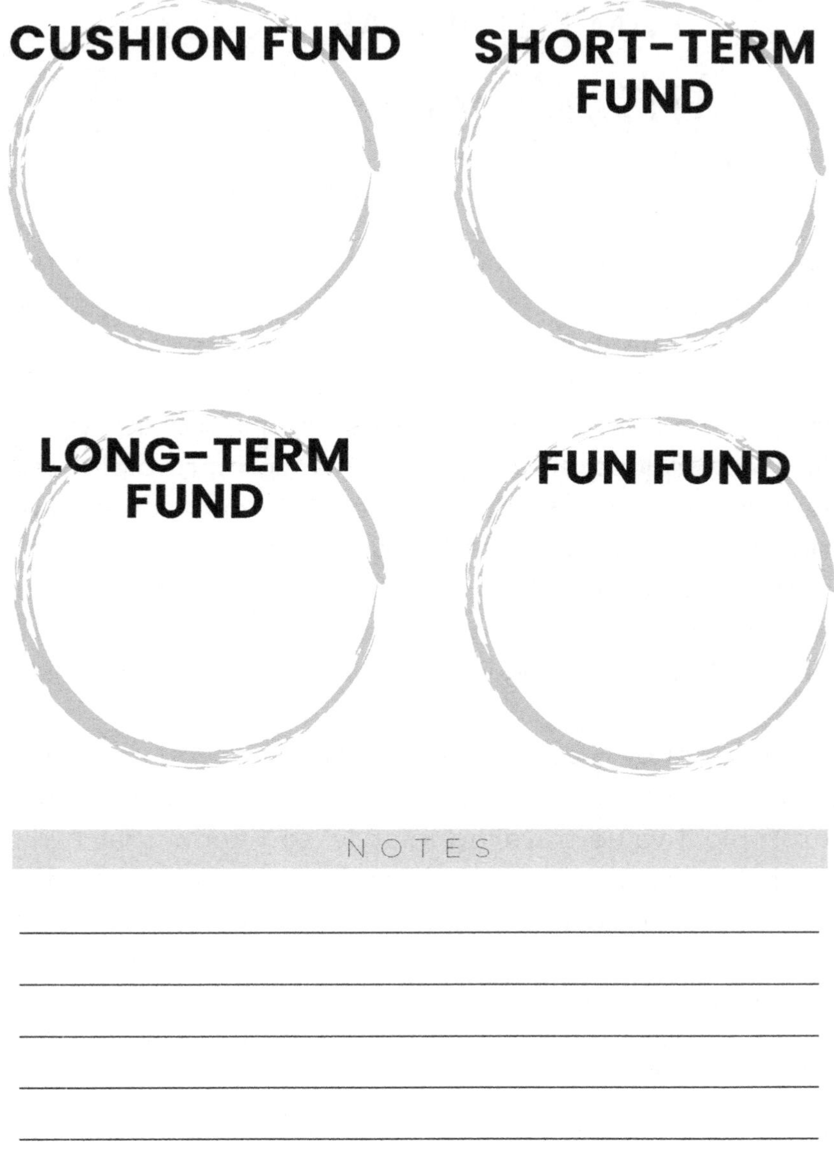

NOTES

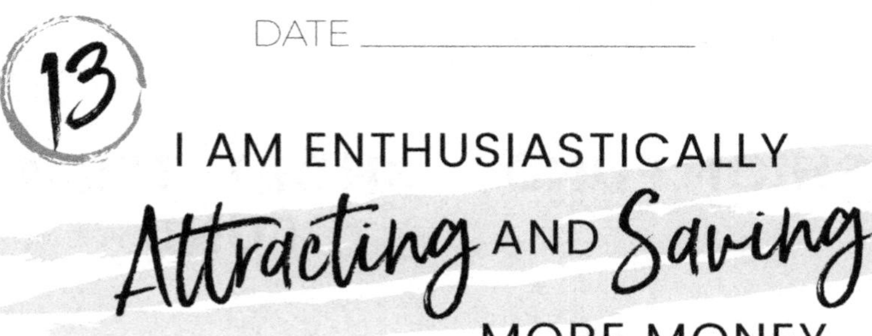

DATE ____________________

13 I AM ENTHUSIASTICALLY *Attracting* AND *Saving* MORE MONEY

Saving money is a choice. It doesn't happen by accident. Most people would love to have a big sum of money sitting in a bank account, but the reality is that nearly 70% of Americans have less than $1,000 stashed away[2]. Why don't people save? It takes committed discipline and continuous effort, which is uncomfortable. Most people get turned off when the 'B' word comes up: budgeting. They imagine budgeting and saving means sacrificing weekends out, never buying anything you like again, having to stay in roach infested motels while on vacation, and living like a miser. That's not true.

Saving money is as easy as knowing what you value the most in life and directing your money towards that. For example, I value traveling in style, so I know that I will definitely spend money on that every year. I'll choose nice accommodations, go to great restaurants and

[2]According to a 2019 GObankingrates poll: https://www.gobankingrates.com/saving-money/savings-advice/americans-have-less-than-1000-in-savings/

COMFORT RATING		**1=** This is complete bullsh*t **10=** I love this! I'm vibing with this, baby!

experience whatever I want. On the other hand, I don't value getting my hair blown out every week (saves me $150+ per month), getting my nails done (saves me $100+), or putting fake eyelashes on my sensitive eyes (saves me $150+). BAM! Those $400 bucks just went into my savings account for my travel fund.

The key is to actively separate and save for what you value the most in your life. You may want the experience of owning your first home, owning your own business, traveling to beautiful places, trying out new restaurants, leaving corporate america, etc. Whatever it is you value, align your money spending with those experiences.

I am enthusiastically attracting and saving more money
I am enthusiastically attracting and saving more money
I am enthusiastically attracting and saving more money
...Repeat 20 times

YOUR TURN:

STEP 1: What type of experiences do I value the most in life? ____

____

____

____

____

____

____

____

STEP 2: Look at 3 months of your credit card statements and see what you've been spending on.

A. What expenses are aligned with your values?

____

____

____

____

____

____

B. What expenses are not aligned with your values?

____

____

____

____

____

____

____

STEP 3: What expenses are you willing to cut per month in order to dedicate that money to the experiences you value most?

____

____

____

____

____

____

NOTES

DATE ____________________

I AM *Grateful* I AM *Trusted* AND I HAPPILY PAY MY BILLS

No one's excited to get bills in the mail. We roll our eyes and see bills as a negative thing, but bills are positive vibes! They're like little testaments of trust in you. A bill means that someone trusted you with a service or product before you actually paid for it! This company or person trusted in your integrity and ability to pay them back. They gave you something based on just your word or signature. You may be thinking, "No, Joyce, they checked my credit and made me sign a loan document saying they can take me to court if I don't pay. That doesn't seem like trust." That's still trust, my friend. You have access to their funds, their product, their service, based on a document.

I don't care how cute and curly or fancy and sophisticated your signature is, it sure as hell ain't worth a $10,000 credit line! Do you know how much work and money is spent having to take someone to court for getting paid back? A company does not want that – they're hoping it won't come to that, which is why they manage their

COMFORT RATING		**1=** This is complete bullsh*t **10=** I love this! I'm vibing with this, baby!

risk by checking credit, however they are still the one taking a risk. So, next time a bill comes in, smile and be grateful someone actually trusted you. Furthermore, think about what each bill represents. When you get a property tax bill, be thankful you own property. Medical bill? Be grateful you're able to find solid healthcare. Rent? Thank your lucky stars you have a place to live. Many people don't have the luxuries you do, so smile & be grateful for your bills :)

I am grateful I am trusted and I happily pay my bills
I am grateful I am trusted and I happily pay my bills
I am grateful I am trusted and I happily pay my bills
...Repeat 20 times

YOUR TURN:

The 1st step to cleaning up your debt is to know where you stand so list the bills, loans, lines of credit, personal loans from family/friends that are still unpaid.

- [ ] ____
  ____
- [ ] ____
  ____
- [ ] ____
  ____
- [ ] ____
  ____
- [ ] ____

- [ ] ______________________________
____
- [ ] ______________________________
____
- [ ] ______________________________
____
- [ ] ______________________________
____
- [ ] ______________________________

Don't fret your debt, my pet. (I'm a poet and I didn't even know it!) Use this information to strategize how you will pay off any debt.

NOTES

____
____
____
____
____
____
____
____
____
____
____
____

15

DATE ____________________

I AM TAPPED INTO THE *Unlimited* UNIVERSAL *Supply* OF MONEY

People make money a 'me and you' thing, but money is a universal flow. Money goes from my hands to yours, then to someone else's, then to someone after that - it is ever flowing as it should be. As *you* make more money, you help *other* people make more money as well. The more you make, the more that circulates to others because of you, hence your success creates success for others.

When you hoard money, you block its flow. Hoarding shows fear and a lack mentality. It's important to save, but there's no need to hoard. When you waste money without a plan, it disrespects its power and purpose.

Money is very similar to a flowing stream of water. If you block the flow of water, the water becomes stagnant, begins to cause rot, and stops feeding vegetation beyond that point. If you direct the stream to places that

COMFORT RATING		**1=** This is complete bullsh*t **10=** I love this! I'm vibing with this, baby!

don't need the water, you are wasting it and what truly needs water will not get enough and die. But if you allow it to flow, and learn to direct the water correctly, it is the biggest blessing to you and to the multitude of people it continues to flow to.

That's my Yoda moment for you – I hope you liked it.

I am tapped into the unlimited universal supply of money
I am tapped into the unlimited universal supply of money
I am tapped into the unlimited universal supply of money
...Repeat 20 times

YOUR TURN:

Is my money flowing where it's needed?
List or draw where your money is flowing to now.

Is there anywhere you want it to flow but it's not?

Is there anywhere it's flowing to but isn't needed?

NOTES

16

DATE ____________________

I AM SO *Grateful* FOR ALL THE ABUNDANCE IN MY *Life*

Have you ever spent time and effort looking for the perfect gift for someone or planning the perfect experience only to have them not appreciate or acknowledge your effort? When this happens, you feel unappreciated and unseen and your desire to give more to this person decreases. On the flip side, did you ever give someone something small and had them appreciate it so much that you feel like doing it again? So, let's use that same concept with this affirmation: If you don't appreciate what you're already blessed with, why would the universe want to give you more? We've been taught to focus on the lack in our lives, to notice what is wrong, to compete, and to constantly want more without enjoying what's already here.

Notice what you already have – you are blessed in your current state. Maybe you don't see it through material goods, but begin to see the abundance in your health, family, friends, the breaths you take, the money you

COMFORT RATING		**1=** This is complete bullsh*t **10=** I love this! I'm vibing with this, baby!

currently make, the opportunity to be here in this moment reading or listening to this book. Who is in your life that enhances your journey? Some of the people in your life are coveted by others. What luxuries are already yours? What you see as 'average' may be a luxury to someone else. What experiences have you had? Some of your experiences are on someone else's wish list. When you are grateful for what's already here, you open yourself up to more abundance. When you express this gratitude, you spread abundance and love in the world – and the world could use some love right now.

I am so grateful for all the abundance in my life
I am so grateful for all the abundance in my life
I am so grateful for all the abundance in my life
...Repeat 20 times

YOUR TURN:

Spend 2 minutes listing all the blessings in your life right now. What people, things, experiences are you grateful for?

____

____

____

____

____

____

____

____

EXTRA CREDIT: *Reach out to 2 of those people today and tell them you are grateful for their presence in your life.*

GRATITUDE GIFT IDEA:

Give this book to someone you care about...or even someone you don't care about cuz they need love too.

NOTES

DATE ____________________

17

I AM HERE TO MAKE AN *Impact.* I HAVE A POWERFUL *Purpose.*

In the vast galaxy of stars, there was a little star who one day realized he didn't shine any brighter than the other stars, wasn't any bigger, wasn't positioned in a meaningful spot, nor was he part of a constellation. Disappointed at his assumed averageness, he asked his maker, "Why am I even here? Nothing makes me special. I'm just like the others." His maker smiled and replied, "Are you sure about that? Look at earth and listen for a moment."

The little star listened intently and began to hear thousands of whispers. "What is that?" asked the little star. "Those are all the people who wish specifically on you every single night. To them, you're more than special, you are hope," his maker replied.

We think we're not a big deal; that we're crazy to believe we have a purpose. We wonder what makes us so special to think we're here for anything bigger, but we miss the possibility that we are here by design. Did you know

COMFORT RATING		**1=** This is complete bullsh*t **10=** I love this! I'm vibing with this, baby!

some studies show the odds of you being born are 1 in 400 trillion? Let's put that into perspective: the chances of you getting struck by lightning is 1 in 500,000. That means you have a higher chance of getting struck by lightning 800 million times, than you do the chance of being born! You are here by design, you are here for a purpose, you are here to impact the people you come across. The fact that you are here, on earth, reading or listening to this book is no mistake – you were designed on purpose, for a purpose. I know sometimes it doesn't feel that way, but just know that your story, your smile, your words, your presence, impacts someone every single day. YOU are a gift.

I am here to make an impact. I have a powerful purpose.
I am here to make an impact. I have a powerful purpose.
I am here to make an impact. I have a powerful purpose.
...Repeat 20 times

YOUR TURN:

List 5 people that impacted your life in a positive way.

1.____

2.____

3.____

4.____

____

____

____

5.____

____

____

List 3 times you were positively impacted by someone you didn't know or barely knew.

1.____

____

____

____

____

2.____

____

____

____

____

3.____

____

____

____

I want you to know that somewhere out there, you are on someone's impact list – YOU have impacted someone enough to make this same list.

NOTES

18

DATE ____________________

I AM GENEROUSLY GETTING *Paid* FOR DOING *What I Love*

Who told you that you can't get paid for doing something you love? Somewhere along the way we were led to believe that life is supposed to be hard, that you have to endure a soulless job to make money, and that following what you enjoy isn't going to pay the bills. If that were true, how does Oprah Winfrey enjoy what she does and make millions doing it? Michael Jordan? Tony Robbins? When you align yourself with something you feel passionate about, you're aligning yourself with your purpose. When you're living in passion and purpose, you feel alive and emit an energy that people are highly attracted to. Case in point: Would you rather do business with a miserable person or someone that's uplifting and energetic? Uplifting and energetic...duh. No one wants to deal with a miserable person for anything.

Aligning yourself with a purpose you're passionate about puts you in the energetic vibration of abundance which then attracts more abundance to you. "But how do I

COMFORT RATING		**1=** This is complete bullsh*t **10=** I love this! I'm vibing with this, baby!

find my purpose?" you're wondering. Here's a starting point:

- Look at the times in your life that you've felt the most alive.
- Think about the causes you feel most strongly about.
- Write down your strengths and how you've impacted people sometimes without even trying.
- Consider your beautiful unique life experiences, both bad and good, what was the purpose behind those experiences? There's a purpose behind everything in your past.

Deep inside, you know what your purpose is, you just have to accept it.

I am generously getting paid for doing what I love
I am generously getting paid for doing what I love
I am generously getting paid for doing what I love
...Repeat 20 times

YOUR TURN:

List 10 times you can think of where you felt the most alive.

1. ____

____

2. ____

____

3. ____

____

4.____

____

5.____

____

6.____

____

7.____

____

8.____

____

9.____

____

10.____

____

What are 2 or more common themes behind these times?

____

____

____

____

____

____

____

You can choose to get deeper into this exercise by answering the questions in the explanation portion of this affirmation as well.

NOTES

19

DATE ______________________

I AM HAPPILY *Enjoying* AND CREATING *Multiple Streams* OF INCOME

As a financial advisor, I'd find it bizarre when people would say, "I don't want all my eggs in one basket" so they'd run around spreading their money, social security number, and private information in several different financial institutions because it made them feel 'safe'. What's funny is that they didn't realize all their eggs were *coming* from just one basket – a corporation or a business - and if that basket was to fail, they'd be screwed. We've been programmed to think of income from one source – our job. That means we're dependent on one entity to feed our family, have a home, pay for our kid's college, go on vacations, and retire happily. All of these cool benefits go away if a jerk boss decides to get rid of you or if the corporation you work for decides to cut costs and lay people off.

This is why it's important to have multiple streams of income rather than just one. Some examples of this are side hustles, rental properties, house hosting programs

COMFORT RATING		**1=** This is complete bullsh*t **10=** I love this! I'm vibing with this, baby!

like Airbnb, partnering in a business, affiliate marketing, stocks or bonds that provide income, selling items online, or a passion like jewelry making, podcasting, and video editing. Get creative! Having additional sources of income gives you more control over your financial success because if one source of income comes to a halt (think back to Covid times), the other ones can continue to produce. A smart farmer plants more than one fruit tree! Be a smart farmer with your money.

I am happily enjoying and creating multiple streams of income
I am happily enjoying and creating multiple streams of income
I am happily enjoying and creating multiple streams of income
...Repeat 20 times

YOUR TURN:

List all the income streams you currently have.

____

____

____

____

____

____

____

____

____

____

Taking into consideration your passions, strengths, and resources around you, come up with 5 ideas for additional sources of income.

1. ______________________________

2. ______________________________

3. ______________________________

4. ______________________________

5. ______________________________

NOTES

DATE ____________________

I AM EXCITEDLY PURSUING MY *Passion.* I TRUST THAT *Wealth* WILL FOLLOW.

When you have passion for something, you look forward to being immersed in it. Notice how you feel when you do something you enjoy, with someone you love, or doing something that positively impacts others. You feel bliss, peace, happy, purposeful, your creativity is high, ideas flow, you're at the top of your game. Notice how things easily come together during moments like these. This is because you're in the energetic frequency of joy and love which are high vibrational emotions. This high vibrational energy is in sync with the universe, so everything flows in your favor. Yet, you deny yourself this feeling by going through the motions in life, thinking success means hard work and toil, staying in situations that no longer make you happy, staying in a career or job you don't enjoy because you're afraid to try something new and fail.

Don't ignore that inner voice that's asking for change. Listen to that desire to follow your passion and take small

COMFORT RATING		**1=** This is complete bullsh*t **10=** I love this! I'm vibing with this, baby!

steps to pursue it. I'm not asking you to submit your job resignation, but I am asking you to pay attention to what you feel about your current work and to allow yourself to explore the possibility of a new stage of life. This could be a different position within the same career field or a totally new venture. As you research and dabble in this new possibility, see how it makes you feel and how it can be monetized to produce the income you need.

Everything great came from someone following a vision, choosing to take a risk, and believing it could happen.

I am excitedly pursuing my passion. I trust that wealth will follow
I am excitedly pursuing my passion. I trust that wealth will follow
I am excitedly pursuing my passion. I trust that wealth will follow
...Repeat 20 times

YOUR TURN:

If I chose to follow a new career path, what would be the minimum amount of money I need to live a lifestyle I'm content with?

____

____

____

To help you calculate this, list your essential monthly expenses such as mortgage, rent, food, utilities, etc. On the next page is a guide to help you.

EXPENSE	MONTHLY AMOUNT PAID
Mortgage/Rent	
Property Tax/HOA fees/Home Insurance	
Utilities: Electric, Gas, Water	
Cell Phone	
Cable/Internet	
Health Insurance/Life Insurance	
Car Payment & Car Insurance	
Credit Card Debt Monthly Payment	
Student Loan & Other Debt Obligations	
Educations Costs/Day Care	
Groceries	
Other	
Other	
MONTHLY TOTAL	

Take this monthly amount and multiply it by 12 to get the annual amount.

_________________ **X 12 =** _________________

This is your baseline income. You need to make this amount in side hustles or multiple streams of income in order to pay your necessities while you pursue your passion career. You can also see this as the amount you need to save in order to have a year's worth of expenses while pursuing a new venture.

NOTES

DATE ____________________

I AM WHO *I Choose* TO BE

If your money, house, materials, titles, roles you play, education level, and accomplishments were all taken away from you tomorrow, who would you be? I challenge you to think about that for a moment.

A NY Times article shed light on the sharp rise in suicide during the Great Recession. They cited a medical journal where "researchers found that the rate [of suicide] between 2008 and 2010 increased four times faster"[3]. It went on to state that for every 1% increase in unemployment, there was a 1% increase in suicide. The stress of losing a paycheck or a home is overwhelming but if you add the devastation of losing your identity, it becomes even more severe. Because we identify ourselves with our accomplishments, materials owned,

[3] https://www.nytimes.com/2012/11/05/health/us-suicide-rate-rose-during-recession-study-finds.html

COMFORT RATING		**1=** This is complete bullsh*t **10=** I love this! I'm vibing with this, baby!

and titles, it can be depressing if they are taken away overnight. Society has taught us to define ourselves with outside things. We work towards accumulating material goods, titles, certificates, money, and accolades in the hopes of feeling enough, adequate, successful, and loved. Yet even with these successes, we often still feel 'something' is missing, so we continue our quest to accumulate. But our titles and net worth do not equal our identity. We are not defined by these outside things. Who we are is defined by our inner world, not the outer world. You are the values you stand for and embody. *You are who you choose to be*, not who society says you *should* be.

This possibility that a rise in suicide could come right after the pandemic of 2020 is what inspired me to speak heavily on the topic of money mindset. I began spreading financial information, inspiration and shifting the mindset around the chaos in hopes of easing the fear, anxiety and desperation I saw in my tribe and community. I want to shift the way we see money, the way we see ourselves, and the way we see the world because the relationship between those 3 things highly impacts our lives and the lives of those around us.

I am who I choose to be
I am who I choose to be
I am who I choose to be
...Repeat 20 times

YOUR TURN:

What values do you stand for? Check off the values you feel strongly about. Then circle your top 5.

Authenticity
Achievement
Adventure Authority
Autonomy
Balance
Beauty
Boldness
Compassion
Challenge
Citizenship
Community
Competency
Contribution
Creativity
Curiosity
Determination
Fairness
Faith
Fame
Friendships
Fun
Growth
Happiness
Honesty
Humor
Influence
Inner Harmony
Justice

Kindness
Knowledge
Leadership
Learning
Love
Loyalty
Meaningful Work
Openness
Optimism
Peace
Pleasure
Poise
Popularity
Recognition
Religion
Reputation
Respect
Responsibility Security
Self-Respect
Service
Spirituality
Stability
Success
Status
Trustworthiness
Wealth
Wisdom

NOTES

DATE ____________________

I Am SUCCESSFUL. I AM WORTHY. I AM Enough.

A businessman passed a merchant selling precious metals on a corner. The businessman grabbed one of the metals and asked its price. To his surprise, the price for this precious metal was less than half of its real worth. The businessman wondered if the precious metal was real or if this was some type of scam. He was skilled in this business, so he tested it and was surprised that it was indeed authentic pure gold. He asked the merchant, "why in the world are you selling pure gold for aluminum prices?!" The merchant's eyes widened in disbelief as he said, "This is gold?! I had no idea!"

If you don't know your worth, you will sell yourself short like the foolish merchant selling gold for aluminum prices. You need to know, see and claim your value. You are the one who sets your value; if you depend on someone else to set it for you, they could be wrong and value you less than what you're truly worth. Don't rely

COMFORT RATING		**1=** This is complete bullsh*t **10=** I love this! I'm vibing with this, baby!

on anyone else's approval or opinion of you. The opinion and validation that truly matters is *your own*. Recognize your successes, see the perfection in your imperfection, embrace yourself as you are today. You are enough exactly as you are. You are gold.

I am successful. I am worthy. I am enough.
I am successful. I am worthy. I am enough.
I am successful. I am worthy. I am enough.
...Repeat 20 times

YOUR TURN:

Write down what makes you a badass! What do you admire, like, or love about yourself?

___

___

___

___

___

___

___

___

___

___

___

What do others tell you that they like, love and admire about you? What makes you different?

NOTES

23
DATE
I Love Myself
JUST THE WAY I AM

Accepting abundance in your life begins with accepting yourself. I repeat: Accepting abundance in your life, begins with accepting yourself. Before you can attract money, abundance, your dream business, a great career, or an amazing hot and loving partner, you need to feel that *you deserve it*. This feeling starts with loving yourself – and I'm talking about every little piece of you. Love and accept your flaws, your extra weight, your uneven eyebrows, your messy past, your oversized cranium, your mistakes and experiences, your big nose... just accept it. All of these things make you perfectly imperfect and it is beautiful...YOU are beautiful. Your story is beautiful. You are one of a kind – love you, embrace you, and know that there is no one else out there with the essence you bring.

I love myself just the way I am
I love myself just the way I am
I love myself just the way I am
...Repeat 20 times

COMFORT RATING		**1=** This is complete bullsh*t **10=** I love this! I'm vibing with this, baby!

YOUR TURN:

I dare you to get naked... NOW... and look in the mirror. Stare at yourself and just begin to accept what you see and feel. You don't have to like it, just accept it. If you feel discomfort, stay in it and just notice what feelings come up. Journal below whatever you felt during this exercise.

NOTES

EXTRA CREDIT: *Look at yourself naked in the mirror and say 10 times: I love you just the way you are.*

24

DATE ____________

I AM *Worthy* OF FINANCIAL *Abundance* AND WELCOME IT INTO MY LIFE

I don't care if you grew up rich, poor, or middle class... if you're black, white, brown, yellow, or blue. I don't care about your religion, gender, education level, or sexual orientation. I don't care how smart you are with money or if you've made awful mistakes with it in the past. You can make money. You *will* make money. You *can* be successful. You *will* be successful. Some of us block our abundance inflow because we are stuck in a label - a label we've placed on ourselves or one placed on us by society. This label limits us to what society sees as acceptable or viable for our label, but it only limits you if you allow it to. Do not let this negative thought process seep into your head because if you do, it can slowly become a crutch or a scapegoat. The more you blame outside factors for your current situation, the more power you lose to them.

Does sexism exist? Yes. Does racism exist? Yes. Is there prejudice? Yes. I've experienced all of them as a Latina woman working in the investment industry, but I refused to let it dictate my belief about what was possible for

COMFORT RATING		**1=** This is complete bullsh*t **10=** I love this! I'm vibing with this, baby!

me. Realistically, we live in a world of labels, class and caste systems but here's how to shift the power to you: see the obstacle and come up with a game plan on how you're going to move past it. Game plan didn't work? Try again. Didn't work again? Try differently. Have you ever seen Lebron throw a hissy fit and complain that the opposing team is pressing on him too hard or guarding him like he's the only player on the court? Nope. He knows what he's up against and he figures out how he's going to win anyway. You are playing the game of life. Yes, there are forces that may oppose your success or make it more challenging but the key is to find the strategy to succeed and keep going. You *deserve it*, you can *create it* and you *will* make it happen!

I am worthy of financial abundance and welcome it into my life
I am worthy of financial abundance and welcome it into my life
I am worthy of financial abundance and welcome it into my life
...Repeat 20 times

YOUR TURN:

OBSTACLE: What would you say is currently in the way of your success or wealth? Think about societal, situational, emotional, educational, medical, etc. - any type of challenge you may be seeing as a block to your success.

GAME PLAN: What would you have to do to move around that obstacle?

What team members might you need?

What 2 steps could you take by the end of this week to act on that game plan?

NOTES

DATE ____________________

Money ALWAYS IMPACTS MY LIFE IN Positive WAYS

Somewhere along the way, we were taught that money is bad, evil, or shouldn't be loved. Maybe we saw our parents fight over money, we've argued with significant others about it, don't have enough of it, have been stabbed in the back for money... whatever little horror story you have in your head about money, today we will let that go. Money is a wonderful thing. It is a very needed tool in our current society, and it should be embraced. It is used every day to help and care for millions of people around the world. You use it to pay for food, water, health care, the homes you live in, education, clothing, transportation, vacations and experiences that create lasting memories. Even taxes which most people dislike paying, are used to pay for repaving roads, social security, medicare, and military.

Money is a positive benefit in your life if you know how to make it, manage it, grow it, and give it. The more money

COMFORT RATING		**1=** This is complete bullsh*t **10=** I love this! I'm vibing with this, baby!

you have, the more you can give and create experiences for yourself and others. Money is a blessing because it is the tool you use to create the experiences you desire.

Money always impacts my life in positive ways
Money always impacts my life in positive ways
Money always impacts my life in positive ways
...Repeat 20 times

YOUR TURN:

List 3 ways your money has positively impacted your loved ones or/and society.

1.____

2.____

3.____

List 3 ways money has positively impacted you.

1.____

2.____

3.____

NOTES

DATE ____________

I AM *Fully* OPEN TO *Give* AND *Receive*

Abundance is an energetic balanced flow of giving and receiving. When you receive, you accept the flow of abundance *into your life*. When you give, you create the flow of abundance out unto others' lives. Giving and receiving freely, allows all involved to experience the joy and completeness of both sides.

Many people have challenges with receiving - they feel uneasy asking for or accepting help because they're ashamed they can't do it themselves, feel like they're 'bothering' someone, or don't want to owe anyone anything. The problem here is that if you're uncomfortable *receiving* from others, you're blocking a pathway the universe can use to deliver abundance to you. Imagine ordering something from Amazon but having no mailbox, no doorbell, and a vicious guard dog circling your home – how in the world do you expect them to deliver your package at your doorstep on time?! We weren't designed to do things alone in this life and

COMFORT RATING		**1=** This is complete bullsh*t **10=** I love this! I'm vibing with this, baby!

there's no prize in the afterlife for people that 'did it all themselves.' It's okay to receive from others. When you receive, you gift someone the pleasure of contributing, feeling needed, and loving you in a way they know how. On the other side of the coin, if you're mostly a taker, you rob yourself of how it feels to contribute, show love, and create abundance for others.

In both giving and receiving, the feeling of abundance is reinforced within you.

I am fully open to give and receive
I am fully open to give and receive
I am fully open to give and receive
...Repeat 20 times

YOUR TURN:

Check off the box if you agree...

- ☐ I feel uncomfortable receiving gifts
- ☐ I hesitate to ask others for favors when I'm overwhelmed
- ☐ I can ask someone for a small favor but typically not for a big favor
- ☐ Affection makes me feel awkward
- ☐ I feel uncomfortable hearing the words "I love you"
- ☐ Receiving compliments is a bit awkward

If you checked off more than 2,
it's time to practice receiving my friend.

List the last 3 times you gave someone something without reason and without expecting something back?

____

____

____

____

____

____

What was it and Why?

____

____

____

____

How did it make you feel?

____

____

____

____

How did it make them feel?

____

____

____

____

DATE ____________________

I Am FULLY OPEN TO RECEIVING Love

Anabelle was a single mom with a low paying job and a side hustle who reached out to me for coaching. "I'm so ashamed of my finances," she admitted, "I'm in so much debt and I'm about to get evicted! How did I get here? What am I going to do with my kids?" she said between sobs. She was scared, hopeless, and desperate. I knew that I had very little time to make things happen for her so we quickly worked on her finances, a new business strategy, shifting her mindset and energy. One of the tasks I asked her to do is to dedicate 20 to 30 minutes of self-love every day. During this time, she was to be alone and fully present in doing something she loved. She could choose to walk, take a bath, dance naked in a field of daisies...anything that would make her happy. Although it was tough to carve out a time in her crammed schedule, she agreed to do it. Within 3 months of coaching, abundance began to flow in: she landed a higher paying job, her side hustle dramatically

COMFORT RATING		**1=** This is complete bullsh*t **10=** I love this! I'm vibing with this, baby!

picked up, and for the first time in a long time, she had saved enough money to pay 2 months worth of rent.

Why did this simple task of self-love work? By dedicating time to herself, she was sending her conscious and subconscious the message: "I'm worth it and I deserve it." This shifted her energy to one of love, gratitude, receiving, calmness, and joy. Her energy prior to this was one of lack, sacrifice, inadequacy, anxiety, and fear. Anabelle was so busy pouring out all the time that she had forgotten how to receive and be loved. Love and abundance come into your life in various ways: in the form of affection, attention, help, concern, quality time, friendship, money, gifts, encouraging words, mentorship, or a shoulder to cry on. However, to accept it, you need to feel that you deserve it and one way to do that is to love yourself first.

I am fully open to receiving love
I am fully open to receiving love
I am fully open to receiving love
...Repeat 20 times

YOUR TURN:

STEP 1: Make a list of 10 activities you love to do.

1.____

____

2.____

____

3. ____

____

4. ____

____

5. ____

____

6. ____

____

7. ____

____

8. ____

____

9. ____

____

10. ____

____

STEP 2: For the next 7 days, dedicate at least 20 minutes to yourself by completing one of these activities.

TIP TO MAKE IT SPONTANEOUS: *Write each activity on a piece of paper and put them in a jar. Pull one of the papers from the jar every day and do what it tells you.*

NOTES

DATE ____________________

I AM FAIR AND *Honest* IN MY FINANCIAL *Transactions*

Money can hurt people or bless people, but it's not *money* doing the hurting or the blessing, it's the person behind the transaction. How you deal with money can create a positive or negative experience for you and anyone involved, but let's focus on how it affects you. Your integrity with money greatly influences the way you feel about yourself. Honesty in financial transactions increases self-confidence because you see yourself as a person of integrity - someone that can be trusted. The choices you make in your money life, affect you physically, emotionally and spiritually because the energy of your thoughts is *inside* of you. If you know you are doing or have done something that goes against your values, it will eat away at you. You bring your sense of self, thoughts and energy everywhere you go. You deal with money every day in almost every aspect of your life, which is why being honest and fair with your financial transactions will increase your sense of self.

COMFORT RATING [ ]

1= This is complete bullsh*t
10= I love this! I'm vibing with this, baby!

When you make it a practice to deal with integrity and a sincere desire to add more value than what is expected, you open the flow of abundance into your life. Others seek you out when service is needed because they trust you and the quality you stand for. When you bring your best, you have no regrets. If in the past you have not handled your financial transactions with integrity, forgive yourself, clean up your messes, and turn a new leaf. It's important to make a best effort to clean up your messes so that it doesn't hang over your head and drain your energy.

I am fair and honest in my financial transactions
I am fair and honest in my financial transactions
I am fair and honest in my financial transactions
...Repeat 20 times

YOUR TURN:

Here are some questions to reflect on when it comes to financial integrity.

1. What, if any, of my current financial practices make me feel uncomfortable or as if I'm compromising my value system?

____

____

____

____

____

Are there any past financial transactions that make me feel a sense of guilt? If so, list what they are and why.

2. Do I have any unfinished money business? For example, friends or family I still owe money to?

3. What steps can I take to begin cleaning up these items?

NOTES

DATE ____________________

I NOW *Forgive* MYSELF AND OTHERS FOR MY FINANCIAL TROUBLES

Look, we don't always make the best decisions with our money. I've been a financial advisor for over a decade, so you'd think my money moves are amazing, but I've made some sh*tty financial decisions too. We don't always get it right - none of us have a crystal ball to know exactly what's going to happen with the stock market, housing market, or whether our money decisions will work or not. So, let's cut ourselves a break and forgive our past erroneous financial decisions. Let it go. Back when you made those decisions (even if it was yesterday), you didn't know what you know today. We grow and learn every day.

Similarly, if someone else has disappointed, betrayed, or hurt you financially, it is time to let that go too. Everyone does the best they can with the knowledge, skills and experience they have at that moment. Holding on to resentment and guilt is a poison to your body, mind, and spirit... and of course, to your money life as well. Any resentment or guilt you hold will create fear in your decisions and transactions moving forward.

COMFORT RATING		**1=** This is complete bullsh*t **10=** I love this! I'm vibing with this, baby!

Fear leads you to inaction, indecisiveness and illogical financial decisions. Do not allow resentment and guilt from the past to bring down your future. Holding on to resentment, anger, or hurt regarding any money situation will negatively affect you emotionally, physically, and financially. Choose acceptance, forgiveness, and understanding - all else is madness.

I now forgive myself and others for my financial troubles
I now forgive myself and others for my financial troubles
I now forgive myself and others for my financial troubles
...Repeat 20 times

YOUR TURN: FINANCIAL FORGIVENESS LETTERS

All you have to do is *write* these letters, *not* send them out. Allow whatever feelings that show up, to come up but don't wallow in them. Feel them and let them go. The purpose here is to become aware and to release some ill feelings you may have against yourself or others. Write 1 letter per person you feel you need to forgive or accept. You may have to write or read this letter to yourself a number of times before you actually release the resentment. There's a deeper process I take my clients through, but I wanted to keep this exercise as short & sweet as I could.

STEP 1: List 3 crappy money decisions you think you've made or any financial blame you put on yourself.

____

____

____

List 3 people that may have hurt you financially and how.

STEP 2: For the decisions you've made, write out a letter in this format: "I now forgive myself for...{insert what you feel you did or didn't do}...I understand that at that time I {insert what you were feeling, or thought that led you to that decision}. Through this experience I learned that {insert what you've learned about yourself, life, love, and/or money} and I now let it go. I now forgive myself.

STEP 3: For the people that you feel have hurt you, write out a letter in this format: I forgive you {insert person's name here} for {insert what they did}...I understand that you may have/have not...{insert an understanding based on seeing it from the eyes of that person}. Through this experience with you, I learned {insert what you learned about yourself, love, life, and/or money} and I know we shared this experience for a purpose. I now forgive you and I let it go.

NOTES

DATE ____________________

I AM SURROUNDED BY EMPOWERING *People* THAT *Prosper Me* EVERY DAY, IN EVERY WAY

Don't complain about the people in your life when you're the one choosing them. If you choose to be around people that criticize, take advantage of you, or rob you of precious energy, it is not them at fault – it is you for choosing to keep them around. You may be thinking, "Wait, Joyce, I was born into a family of energy vampires – how is that my fault?" It's no one's fault, but it's a choice. YOU choose who you allow into your mind and how much airtime you give them. You can choose to spend less time with people that bring you down or create drama. The less airtime you give someone, the less they can affect you. If you can't physically stay away from this person, give what they say and do less airtime in your head.

It is your choice on whether negative people affect your energy and mindset. Are you going to entertain their bullsh*t and bring yourself down in the process? OR are you going to dodge their negativity like a ninja? What's worked for me is keeping the convo short with

COMFORT RATING		**1=** This is complete bullsh*t **10=** I love this! I'm vibing with this, baby!

people that complain, criticize or just give off bad juju. Another thing that works is to shift the conversation to something more positive – if they want to bring it back to the negative, excuse yourself from the conversation. There's a difference between lending a friend a shoulder to cry on once in a while and being their full-blown therapist.

Surround yourself with people that inspire you, love you, challenge you to grow, and want you to prosper. Find these people, seek them out and add value to their lives the same way they add value to yours.

I am surrounded by empowering people that prosper me every day, in every way
I am surrounded by empowering people that prosper me every day, in every way
I am surrounded by empowering people that prosper me every day, in every way
...Repeat 20 times

YOUR TURN:

It's time to take inventory of the people in your life. On the next page you'll find a chart.

STEP 1: Write down the 7 people you spend the most time with in your personal and work life.

STEP 2: Put a if they brighten your day, if they're typically a downer, if they're somewhere in the middle.

STEP 3: Jot down a couple of adjectives on how each person makes you feel.

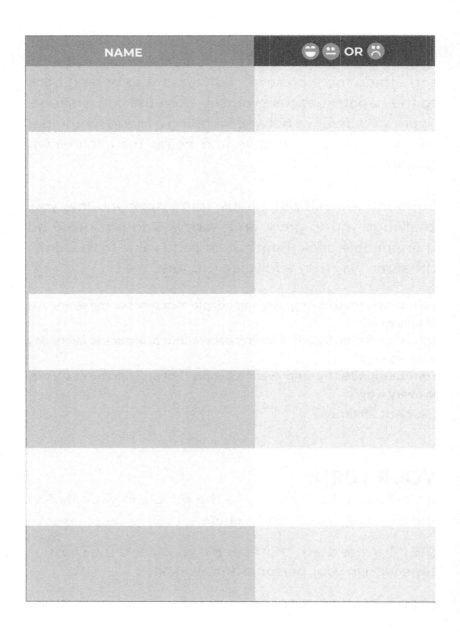

NAME	😀 😐 OR ☹️

STEP 4: Spend less or no time with the downers, more time with the brighteners, and consider swapping out the neutrals. This makes space to add cool, positive vibing people and mentors.

31

DATE ____________________

I AM READY TO *Embrace* MY BEAUTY, *Power*, AND PURPOSE

There is a unique beauty in you that only *you* possess. That's right. No one else. Look at the tip of your finger, observe the lines, pattern, curves of your fingerprint. No one on earth has that same fingerprint. Only you. As unique as your fingerprint, is the story and purpose you bring to this earth. All the wins you've had, the challenges you've overcome, tears you've cried, smiles you've given, laughs you've shared – all of these experiences are yours. No one could have created these moments with the people you've encountered the way YOU did. No one. Your uniqueness, the experiences you've created for others, and the feelings you've inspired in others is your true legacy. There's beauty in your story, power in your purpose, and impact in your legacy. It is time you notice that. It is time you embrace that. It is time you share it with the world. You are beautiful, powerful and impactful and you are here for a grand purpose.

COMFORT RATING		**1=** This is complete bullsh*t **10=** I love this! I'm vibing with this, baby!

I am ready to embrace my beauty, power, and purpose
I am ready to embrace my beauty, power, and purpose
I am ready to embrace my beauty, power, and purpose
...Repeat 20 times

YOUR TURN:

What did you learn in these last 31 days? Take some time to journal what you learned.

What I learned about myself is...

What I learned about money is...

What I learned about the world is...

NOTES

END OF AFFIRMATIONS

JUST *Kidding!*

I know the book says
"31 Badass Affirmations" but I'm the author and I can do what I want, so I've decided to give you bonus ones and make it 35! What can I say? I'm a badass chick and that's how I roll. So, here's 4 more to empower your mind.

DATE ____________________

I AM *Connected* TO THE ABOUNDING *Energy* OF MONEY

Everything in the world is made up of energy – we are energy and so is money. You can energetically attract money or repel it by the way you think, feel, and act around money. Your beliefs about money, yourself, and the world will determine whether money is energetically attracted to you or not. If you believe people with money are greedy, then you will not attract money into your life! Money is a blessing – it is just a tool to enhance your experience here on earth.

Let go of the idea that money doesn't work in your favor, you're not good at handling it, or any idea that gives a negative connotation to money. Money is simply a tool you use to enhance your time here on earth. You use your feet to take you places and your eyes to see beautiful things – they enhance your experience here on earth. Technically, you can live without them, but

COMFORT RATING		**1=** This is complete bullsh*t **10=** I love this! I'm vibing with this, baby!

life would be a totally different experience. Similarly, money is used to help you create experiences that you desire in this lifetime. You can live without it, but you'd be experiencing a completely different life. Money is not a bad thing – it has no negative energy or power over you. It is a friend that can work with you to create a multitude of experiences while you inhabit earth during this lifetime.

I am connected to the abounding energy of money
I am connected to the abounding energy of money
I am connected to the abounding energy of money
...Repeat 20 times

YOUR TURN:

What type of energy have I been bringing to my financial life? Circle the ones that match.

FEAR	RESPONSIBILITY	ANXIETY	WORRY
ACCOUNTABILITY	DISREGARD	DECISIVENESS	THOUGHTLESSNESS
VANITY	ACTION	AIMLESS	CLARITY
IRRESPONSIBILITY	GRATITUDE	INDECISIVENESS	THANKLESSNESS
FAITH	PURPOSE	DIRECTION	CONTROL

33

DATE ____________________

I AM *Decisive* AND TAKE *Action* WITH MY FINANCES

Do you know that your finances need work, but you just don't want to deal with it right now? You decide, "I'll deal with it later," but there's never an opportune 'later' moment that comes. Indecisiveness and procrastination are easy traps to fall into when it comes to finances. Once you fall into this cycle, you begin to lose confidence, power, and opportunity. Every time you're indecisive, you're basically telling yourself, "I don't trust my decision making." This becomes a negative affirmation which is the opposite of what you're trying to do with this book (just sayin'!). Here's a little secret: One small action step gets the ball rolling. You may be afraid of making the 'wrong decision' but with every decision you either take steps towards your goal or you learn from it – both are wins. Life is about taking calculated risks – it is not about avoiding mistakes. You have the logic and intuition to make great decisions and take powerful action in your financial life. And remember, if you need some advice, take action and find the right people to help you.

COMFORT RATING ☐

1= This is complete bullsh*t
10= I love this! I'm vibing with this, baby!

I am decisive and take action with my finances
I am decisive and take action with my finances
I am decisive and take action with my finances
...Repeat 20 times

YOUR TURN:

What actions or decisions have you been avoiding or procrastinating on in your financial life? List 3 things you've been avoiding or procrastinating on and why.

1.____

____

____

____

____

2.____

____

____

____

____

3.____

____

____

____

____

What's 1 step you can take today to get that started?

Who can hold you accountable to finish this?

NOTES

34

DATE ____________________

I AM *Intuitively* GUIDED IN *Creating* WEALTH AND PROSPERITY

It's scary to feel like you're making financial decisions alone. You ask yourself, "Is this the right decision? What if I'm wrong? What should I do?" You go around asking 100 different people what they would do, only to get 100 different answers. Use the power of your inner guidance to lead you. Higher spirit can guide your finances by sending an intuitive message, the right mentor, or signs that'll help you find the answer you are seeking, but the trick is to *listen* and *take action*. If your finances are not thriving, then do something about it! If you need more knowledge, then seek it out. You need a mentor or professional, find one. You have the power to make a change in your life. You can practice the law of attraction, pray to God every night, get energy healing, go to psychics, get your oracle cards read but it means *nothing* if you don't take action towards your goals.

Many people live in this 'God will provide' mentality without taking responsibility for their own actions and

COMFORT RATING		**1=** This is complete bullsh*t **10=** I love this! I'm vibing with this, baby!

inaction. All this does is shift the responsibility and blame to God and away from them under the guise of spirituality. How convenient. Listen, I'm a big God believer, but I know that God isn't here to do my work for me. I can turn to God for guidance and strength, but I surely don't expect God to solve my problems if I'm not doing anything about it. So next time you rely on God or the universe, just picture God looking down at you asking, "You want me to fix your finances? Well, what the heck are you doing about it?" Don't use God, the universe, or your spirituality as a scapegoat for YOUR not taking smart actions with your money.

I am intuitively guided in creating wealth and prosperity
I am intuitively guided in creating wealth and prosperity
I am intuitively guided in creating wealth and prosperity
...Repeat 20 times

YOUR TURN:

Below are 5 people that are game changers to your money life. Jot down who fills each of these 5 spots.

If you don't have someone in a category, find someone.

1. Accountant ________________________________

2. Money Mentor/ Financial Advisor____________________

3. Lawyer________________________________

4. Mastermind Group____________________

5. Coach /Mentor____________________

NOTES

DATE ____________________

I Prosper IN LOVE HEALTH AND WEALTH

When people tell you, "Money can't buy you love," "Money isn't important," or "Money doesn't make you happy", they're not telling you the whole story. Not only do I see these statements as unfinished sentences, but I also find that the people saying them typically don't have money or had a lot of money but didn't balance their life well and now regret it. I'm keeping it real here. Yes, hearing these types of things are great in a moment where you need a pep talk, but they restrict abundance; they give the idea that wealth is unnecessary and that it's noble to only want love and health.

Denying wealth is not noble, it doesn't make you more spiritual, nor does it make you a better person. It's okay to want wealth. We were made to have all of the above. You can have health, love AND money all at the same time – you don't have to choose one over the other. Love is the core of who we are, health is needed to keep us alive, and wealth is the means to create the amazing experiences we desire. All 3 can be balanced in a way that brings body, mind and spirit together – and that is a beautiful thing.

COMFORT RATING		**1=** This is complete bullsh*t **10=** I love this! I'm vibing with this, baby!

I prosper in love, health and wealth
I prosper in love, health and wealth
I prosper in love, health and wealth
...Repeat 20 times

YOUR TURN:

Here's your chance to be a kid again and imagine! Imagine how it would look for you to be prospering in your financial life. How would it look to prosper in health, love and wealth all at once? How does it feel? Where are you? What's happening around you? Who are you with? Imagine this vision and write it down.

EXTRA CREDIT: *Imagine this for 60 seconds or more every day for a full week. See what intuitive ideas or action steps pop in your head. When something pops up, take ACTION! This is your mind and spirit helping you make it a reality.*

NOTES

I want to thank you for taking this 31 (but really 35) day journey with me. I suspect that some of these affirmations made you feel a little uncomfortable—they were designed to. One of the things I've learned from helping so many clients empower themselves around money, is that their perception of 3 concepts will highly affect how money works (or doesn't) in their life. Ask yourself these 3 questions:

1. What do I believe about the World? (W)
2. What do I believe about Myself? (M)
3. What do I believe about Money? ($)

If you believe the world is working for you rather than against you, you'll naturally be more open to opportunity and abundance. If you believe you're competent at managing money and that you deserve it, you're more likely to make confident decisions, take action, and allow yourself to accumulate it. If you believe money is a positive experience in your life and that it's plentiful, then you'll accept it and create ways to accumulate it rather than push it away. These 3 concepts work very tightly together in your money mindset and need to be programmed correctly for you to be open to wealth and abundance. I know I mentioned this in one of the affirmations you practiced, but I want to reinforce how important it is. Now, you may be wondering "How do I know which one of these mindset factors I'm having trouble with?"

Well, surprise, surprise! Your girl Joyce got you. I sneakily put icons on every affirmation to help you out with this.

- ☐ Go back and see which affirmations you were most uncomfortable with based on your 'comfort level' ratings. These are affirmations your subconscious likely had trouble believing or accepting
- ☐ Check what icon is at the bottom right-hand side of each of those uncomfortable affirmations. It could be a W, M, or $ icon.
- ☐ Which icon came up for you the most?

____

The W's:

If 'W' came up most for you, it's likely that the way you view the world is holding you back from abundance, so delve into those beliefs. Do you believe the world works for you or against you? Do you believe people are here to help you, teach you, or hurt you? Do you believe there is abundance or scarcity? Unity or division? What do you believe about the world and its dynamics?

The M's:

If you got mostly "M', then the way you see yourself may be holding you back from financial abundance. Delve into questions like: Do I feel like I deserve abundance? Do I trust myself to run my own finances? Am I good enough to have everything I desire? Am I scared of wealth because it means changing what I'm familiar with now? Am I afraid to leave someone behind if I become successful? Do I truly deserve happiness and love? Am I here for a purpose? Am I enough right now?

The $'s:

If you mostly chose '$', then the way you see money is holding you back. Delve into; Do I see money as a good thing or a bad thing in my life? How about in the world? Is money hard or easy to make? Is there a lot of it or a little? How do I feel about people with money? Does money scare me or excite me? Do I feel money connects with spirituality or are they against each other?

Whatever icon came up the most, is the mindset factor I'd encourage you to delve into and work on, because this feeling of resistance is typically a sign of subconscious insecurities lurking in your mind. I thought that would be a cool little treasure hunt activity I gave you just as you thought you were done with the book!

I would encourage you to practice these affirmations and go through the full 31 days at least twice, preferably consecutively. Since you're pelting your subconscious mind with new beliefs, you need to be consistent for them to stick. I would also highly recommend taking action on the exercises you did. The exercises were designed to help you see your financial picture, understand yourself, and decide what you want to create at this moment in time. The really cool thing about this book is that you can get another copy of it 3 months from now, do the affirmations and exercises again, and find that your answers and reactions are different from the first go around.

TIP: *Get your partner their own book!*
It's a great way to learn things about each other that you never knew. Have fun with it because money doesn't have to be so damn serious!

Round 2
Tips & Tricks

If you're an awesome overachiever who's done the 31 days consecutively and you're ready for round 2, then here are some advanced tips you can use while doing your affirmations.

1. Evolve them to your liking

You can evolve your affirmations by adding more of your own personality, energy, and words to it. Take yourself through a happy thought process of affirming yourself and see if you come up with a different affirmation that you like better.

Here's an example of how I personally evolve an affirmation (this is literally what goes through my head, so don't judge):

Every financial decision I make multiplies my income
Every financial decision I make multiplies my income
I'm talking EVERY financial decision I make multiplies my income
*Every financial decision I've made has already multiplied my income in some way, so I'm amazing at this sh*t!*
I know what I'm doing. I AM AMAZING at making financial decisions
I'm a financial decision maverick!

Go Joyce, Go Joyce, I'm amazing, I'm amazing {as I do my happy dance}
I am a money maverick and every financial decision I make always multiplies my income!

See how I played with that until I came up with a new and improved affirmation at the end? Notice how the feeling in the last affirmation is stronger than the first one. You gotta psych yourself up! Be your own cheerleader – that's how excited I want you to get with your affirmations. You need to feeeeeeel it, baby! The emotion you bring in will make it more real and this tricks your mind into believing what you are saying. It also energetically puts you in the right vibration to attract what you want. Try it, it's fun. Personally, I like to do it when I'm alone in the car so that no one finds out how crazy I am.

2. Visualize It, baby!

This one is very powerful. Your brain and body don't know the difference between what's really happening or what you're imagining. For example, did you ever have great sex with someone and then months later still remember it as if it were yesterday? As you remember it, you're visualizing it and you begin to become aroused all over again – your heart beats faster, you breathe deeper, your body starts feeling hotter – this is a biological reaction to your thoughts. You're not actually there having sex with your past hot partner, you're just remembering it, but your body doesn't know the difference. Your mind is simulating an experience and your body is reacting to it. Now check out what happens... If you keep replaying this in your head, guess what you'll want to do? You'll want to experience it again, but hmmm, you haven't spoken to this person in months... is this do-able? Doesn't matter - the visualization is so intense that you now want to re-create this experience so you hit up your past partner and see if they're available.... maybe tonight? Your brain just made you take deliberate action because the visualization kept motivating other parts of your brain to create what you wanted. That is the power of the mind.

You may be wondering, "But how do I do that with things I haven't experienced yet like being wealthy or having a house on the beach?" It's the same concept. Your mind doesn't know the difference between reality and imagination so as long as you visualize what you want long enough, give it some feeling, and really get into it, your brain will begin to figure out how to make it happen because your body is now craving it.

3. Use a power stance

Okay, I'm a big Wonder Woman fan, I'm just gonna put that out there right now. I love standing like Wonder Woman – it makes me feel powerful. Affirmations work better when your body and mind collaborate because it becomes both a mental and physical experience. Who was your favorite superhero when you were a kid? Stand like your favorite superhero and say your affirmations aloud. If you have kids, have them do it with you – they'll love it. If you're not feeling the power pose, then just use your body in some way to give it more feeling. You can do a happy dance while saying your affirmations, put your hands on your chest when you say, "I am", pump your fist like you're dancing at a NJ club down the shore – just get creative and enjoy it.

How to make your own affirmations

Affirmations are a very personal thing. One size does not fit all. I believe the best type of affirmations are ones that you tweak to your liking or write out for yourself because it gives you an opportunity to express your vision in words. When you personalize your affirmations, you are choosing what you want to see in your future, what you want to create in your life, what you want to be, until the day you see it come to fruition. You can create affirmations as powerful statements that help embed a belief as truth in your mind to empower you. An example of this is, "I am a powerful money master" or "Everything always works in my favor." You can also create affirmations as statements of action that help you visualize an experience you want to manifest in your life. An example would be, "I am happily enjoying multiple streams of income." Both types of affirmations are powerful in helping you shift your mindset, so here are some guidelines on how to create your own...

1. Use 'I am' to empower you

'I am' is a very powerful statement because the subconscious takes it as a command. This is why anytime you say the words 'I am', it's best to follow it with something positive. Not every affirmation needs to start with 'I am' but I've found that it's a springboard to easily creating empowering affirmations. Stating 'I am' also serves as a reminder that affirmations are designed for you and your actions, not for the actions of others. You do not control the actions and decisions of others so make sure that your affirmation speaks of what *you* are doing, receiving, or experiencing.

EXAMPLE:

I am happily receiving $5,000 in child support and alimony from my ex-husband.

I am happily receiving $5,000 monthly from multiple streams of income

Notice that the second affirmation empowers you because it takes you from relying on your ex husband to relying on yourself and the multitude of possibilities to create income.

2. State it in the positive

Your affirmation should describe what you *want* rather than what you don't want. We're very accustomed to speaking in negative terms that state what we do not want. For example, we'll tell our kids, "Do not be messy" rather than saying, "Be neat", we say, "I don't want debt" rather than saying "I want to be financially free", we think about not living 'paycheck to paycheck' rather than envisioning living 'in abundance and financial stability'. Begin stating and thinking in positive end results.

TIP: If you see the word 'not', 'no', or any word that describes what you don't want, remove it and rephrase.

EXAMPLE:

✗ I am no longer in debt
Notice that you still have the word 'debt' in there so your brain and the universe hear 'debt' and decide, "sounds like she wants more debt, let's make that happen!" Therefore, state what you want to create.

✓ I am now proudly financially free

3. Use an action word in the present

You want this affirmation to be stated in the present, and not the future. A great way to stay in the present is to use an action verb ending with '-ing' like: enjoying, making, traveling, investing.

If you state your affirmation in the future, then your reality will always be in the future and not in the present. It will be like a carrot on a stick, right in front of you but unattainable.

EXAMPLE:

✗ I am going to be wealthy

✓ I am enjoying my wealth

4. Use a feeling word

Try to add a feeling word in there so that it helps you visualize the affirmation taking place. If the affirmation is too dry and boring, it won't inspire you. We are inspired by the feeling that an experience will bring us. This is personal preference as I don't use a feeling word in every affirmation because I like to keep them short and evolve them as I'm saying them. However, if your imagination isn't as active as mine or you're new to this, try using a feeling word in your affirmations.

EXAMPLE:

I am enjoying my wealth

With feeling word: I am blissfully enjoying my wealth.

5. Keep it short & specific

Maybe it's because I grew up in a fast-paced city life and want every moment to count, but I like to keep my affirmations short so that it's easier to remember on the go. Remembering them, makes it easy for you to repeat aloud or in your head while you drive, walk, take the train, or use the potty. Think efficiently. Also, make sure you're being specific by stating important details that matter.

EXAMPLE:

I am making more money
If you make $100 more this year than last year, technically you just made more money but I doubt that's what you had in mind with this affirmation. So, here's a better route...

I am joyfully making $200,000 a year

Remember that these are *guidelines,* not a math formula written in stone. All your affirmations do not need to be structured exactly like this and you'll notice that the affirmations in this book do not follow all 5 guidelines all the time. Straying from a guideline in order to make it resonate with you is okay. Personally, I like variety in my affirmations and choose feeling over formula. I would say the must haves are stating in the positive and staying in the present, but other than that you are free to go wild creating affirmations that speak to you.

YOUR TURN:

Go back to the exercises you did for affirmations #1 and #2 where you stated what you wanted to create in your life and financial life. Write these visions as affirmations following the guidelines.

I am honored that you have made me part of your money mindset journey. I believe my calling is to empower people to see the beauty, power, and purpose within themselves and their lives. I hope I have done that for you. Many people wonder how to find and follow their purpose in the next stage of their life. They often ask me what led me to follow my purpose of inspiring people through speaking, teaching, and writing. I'll share my intimate story on the life changing event that led me to follow my purpose in the next couple of pages, but before I do that, here's how you can continue empowering your money mindset and help others as well:

- [ ] Go to **www.joycerojas.com** and sign up to be part of my tribe. I give a ton of free information and educational videos. You'll also be the first to find out about upcoming coaching courses or events

- [ ] Gift a copy of this book to others. This raises the awareness and vibration of the people around you, and in the world.

- [ ] Review this book on amazon or any book sites so that more people can find it.

The near-death experience that changed my life

"You think you're living life, but you're really sleepwalking through it. On the brink of it being taken away, it could be too late to wake up." Joyce Rojas

I'm a big believer that we are all here for a purpose. We may not recognize what that purpose is or have come into perfect alignment with it yet, but I can assure you that you and I are not here by mistake. You and I are here by beautiful design. I learned this the hard way and I want to share it with you so that you may be spared experiencing this epiphany the severe way I did.

I remember the sunny California day that changed my life and mindset forever – I was smack in the middle of the Great Recession. I worked in the banking industry and it was in total havoc; the housing bubble had burst, stock market had plummeted, banks were failing, and people were losing jobs daily. I had no idea if I'd have a job the next day but most importantly, I was in the middle of a hurtful, messy divorce. My heart was broken, my son's heart was broken, and I felt like my life was falling apart. One day, I dropped my son off and went to work. As I'm working, the electricity shuts off in the building – this has never happened before. I waited a little bit for it to come back on but since it didn't, I decided to step out and grab a cup of coffee from a nearby café. As I walked across the street, I was hit by a pickup truck! I clearly remember the thoughts that went through my head. The first thought was, "Is this it? Was that all there was to my life?" I felt bamboozled. What kind of cruel joke was this? Here I was about to die, and that was my life? I hadn't lived out my purpose and I hadn't truly savored life.

The second thought, and the one that haunted me most was, "What kind of morning did I have with my son that day?" I couldn't remember whether it had been one of those stressful mornings where I rushed him and made him cry with my anxious ways, or a good morning where I left him with a smile on his face. As I lay on the concrete waiting for paramedics, I tried so hard to remember but I couldn't. It bothered me so much. How could I not remember if the person I loved the most in this world had hugged me? How could I not recall the feeling of his small arms around me or whether I had seen his beautiful smile that day? At that moment, I realized that I had been sleepwalking through life – that everything truly important to me was not what I was prioritizing. Why did it take almost losing my life to clearly see what was truly important to me? That day taught me 2 things; I was here for a purpose and I was done sleepwalking through life. That's where my journey began.

Not too long after, I finalized my divorce and decided to go back to New Jersey. I could no longer afford to live in the beautiful house I had, so I had to short sell it and take a big loss. I sold all of my belongings in a garage sale for pennies on the dollar. I sadly watched as my son overpriced his toys in the garage sale because to him, they were worth more than $1. It was hurtful to watch. All I had to my name was a car, my kid, and a cooler in the back seat. I had no idea what I was going to do, how I was going to provide for my son, or how my life would turn out as a single mom. I didn't know whether I could do it all on my own, but as I drove to New Jersey, I kept telling myself it would work out – I fed myself positive thoughts to negate the shitty 'what-if's' that flooded my mind.

When I got to New Jersey, I moved into a small studio apartment the size of a dorm room. I had gone from a three bed, three bath beautiful home in California to a crappy studio in the city. My son and I slept on the same bed because there wasn't much space in the studio. My 'dinner table' was a small garden patio table with 2 mismatched stools to sit on, and my son went from playing on green grass to a concrete parking space in the back of our building. I felt like a loser. I had also taken a financial advisor position that paid waaaaay less than what I was making before, so the struggle was real. There were many times I'd cry in the shower so my son wouldn't hear me. When the fear and doubt would set in while at work, I would hold back the tears as I slipped out of my office and into the bathroom to cry. "WTF did you do Joyce? WTF did you do??!!" I'd angrily ask myself.

I doubted myself, doubted my decisions, feared that my son would turn out all f*cked up because his dad wasn't around much, and I resented not having a partner to run decisions by, grow wealth together, and succeed faster. In time I realized this mindset was all wrong. All of these thoughts were just fears being fabricated into overdramatized stories in my head. These were my 'shitty what-if's' gaining traction and sowing seeds of hopelessness and fear. I began to shift my mindset by catching myself thinking something negative, and then switching it to something hopeful and inspiring. I went from believing I needed a partner to believing in myself, from fabricating shitty what-ifs to creating inspiring possibilities, and from feeling sorry for myself as a single mom to feeling empowered and capable. Being a single mom was no longer a handicap to me, it became a gift. Here I was being placed under so much pressure that I was becoming a diamond. In time, my ex-husband was no longer a foe; he was a teacher sent from the universe to help me discover my powers. My accident was no longer something I resented; it became the kick in the ass I needed to set me in the right direction. I began seeing things differently because I chose to shift my mindset. Within 5 years, I quadrupled my income and assets, got my MBA, aligned myself with my purpose and spent more time than ever before with my son. I was happier, more alive, and my life had color once again.

I am now a transformational speaker on money and mindset. By now, my content has reached and positively impacted thousands of people in an effort to help people see the beauty, power and purpose within. I'm here to inspire you to look at your beautiful life story and connect the dots. To realize that everyone in your path has been sent to teach you something about life, love, or yourself. That your presence, energy, and movement to bettering yourself enhances this world. That you are here by design, to design, and you do so every day.

WITH LOVE,

Joyce Rojas

If this book impacted you, please review it on amazon so that others can find it too. It's your way of contributing to a healthier mindset on earth.

Author Bio

Joyce Rojas has positively impacted thousands of people's lives by shifting their relationship with money. With over 19 years in the banking & investment industry, experience as a top financial advisor at a Fortune 500 company, and a Masters in Business Administration, Joyce is easily a top expert in money matters. But her secret is not in all those accolades, it's in knowing that wealth begins with mindset.

As a Latina in a male dominated industry, a single mom, and daughter of immigrant parents, Joyce had the cards stacked against her. She painfully watched her father exhaust himself working 2 jobs in order to provide for his family. She couldn't understand why making money was so hard for him, yet easy for others. As a struggling single mom, she wanted a different life for her son but found herself living the same scarcity pattern she lived as a child. This frustration led her to delve deep into the factors that truly determine financial success. She discovered that subconscious belief systems and thought patterns around money were what held people back the most. Armed with this knowledge, she now helps others rewire their thoughts around money so they can create the abundance they deserve.

Joyce Rojas is a financial advisor and transformation speaker on money mindset. Her impactful work focuses on helping people take control of their financial lives, gain financial clarity, and create the mindset needed to succeed in life.

Acknowledgments

***"If you want to go fast, go alone.
If you want to go far, go together"***
AFRICAN PROVERB

Writing this book was a journey and I am blessed to have had people in my path that inspired, guided, and motivated me throughout the process. I want to take a moment to thank them for being in my life...

Thank you to my son, Talos. Your presence, love, and belief in me, fuel me more than anything else does. You inspire me to be the best version of myself. I am so proud of you and I love you more than you'll ever know.

Thank you to my mom and dad for your love and presence. I love you, and you truly deserve more appreciation than I express.

Thank you, Patty Aubery, for your inspiration and coaching during this process. Your guidance was indispensable.

To my mentor, Jack Canfield, thank you for sparking and illuminating my growth journey.

Thank you to my mastermind group: Aida, Demo, Garret, Michele, and Molly, for sharing your genius with me, inspiring me to think bigger, and offering your love when I'm running low on motivation.

Thank you to the following people for being indispensable in taking this book to a higher level of badassery by reading and giving their feedback in advance:
Becky A, Joanna B, Minda B, Michael E, Yvonne H, Sarah M, Betsy R, Viviana R, Robyn S, Carmel T, Danielle V, Mara W, Janet W.

Thank you to my creative and talented designer, Margaret Cogswell, for expressing my vision on paper. And to my editor, Rusti Lehay, who kept my book's personality intact while keeping me grammatically correct.

Thank you to all my friends, family members, and social media followers who keep me motivated to continue, through your support and notes of encouragement.

Thank You!

WITH LOVE, Joyce

If you want more of me, visit my website to see what shenanigans I'm up to and sign up for whatever the heck I'm offering. It's always good sh*t.

www.joycerojas.com

Made in the USA
Las Vegas, NV
02 September 2021

29409241R00108